An inside look at 12 of the top high school football programs around the country and the states that produce them

GAVIN KRALIK

Foreword by Former NFL Coach, Sam Rutigliano

Gridiron Publishing
1625 E 72nd St, Suite 125
Tacoma, WA 98404

Edited by Kara Hagerman

First Edition: September, 2008

Printed in the United States of America

ISBN 978-0-615-21968-4

Contents

This book is dedicated to five of the coaches who had a major impact on me; Mike Hagadone, Skip Hall, Sam Rutigliano, Pete Sundheim, and Frank Rocco.

Acknowledgements

THERE WERE MANY people who helped to make this book possible. To begin with, I need to thank my wife, Krista, who was patiently supportive throughout the whole process of putting this book together. My sister-in-law, Kara, edited this book alongside me in the midst of a very busy year for her, and to her I am grateful. I would also like to thank my dad who was faithful in reading everything that I sent him and offering feedback as well.

I would also like to express my gratitude to all of the coaches who took time out of their busy schedules and allowed me to learn much from their many years of experience. Without these twelve men taking the time to meet with me, there would be no book. Josh Kranish and Clint Hortman were also very helpful in researching both of their schools. Additionally, there were many people who helped me out with pictures along the way, and to all of them I am very appreciative. I would also like to thank Mike Kersey, who designed all of the helmets for the cover. A special thanks to Carolyn Madison and Jonathan Gullery for their help with the book as well.

I was thrilled to have Sam Rutigliano, someone who had such an impact on my life, write the foreword. My good friend, Don Ferron, is also someone whose friendship I value very much and assisted me in so many different ways that I could not begin to count. Lastly, I am very thankful to Justin Larsen, who worked extra hard during this year's off-season to help build our high school football program while I was so busy writing this book. Without

Justin's extra effort, I would not have been able to continue as head coach this year.

Foreword

"Young people don't care how much you know until they know how much you care."

GAVIN KRALIK HAS written a book on high school football which represents the very best programs in the country. During the course of my career, spanning from 1956–2006, I have coached in high school, college, and the National Football League (NFL). It is amazing that the players who have kept in touch with me were the players who I coached in high school.

As I write this foreword, my wife and I are preparing to attend a fiftieth class reunion at Lafayette High School in Brooklyn, New York, on May 18, 2008. *Newsweek* conducted a study of young people who have been able to climb out of dysfunctional family situations and make it to the top. In each case when the young person succeeded, the common denominator was a coach, teacher, or mentor who was there to connect, direct, and encourage that young person. Heroes change people's lives. Encouragement is the oxygen of the soul. And, it is better to raise a youngster than it is to repair an adult.

What an honor it is for me to write this foreword for a former player of a college where I coached, Liberty University.

—Sam Rutigliano, former NFL Head Coach

Introduction

AS A YOUNG head football coach in the Seattle area, I recognized early in my coaching career that I was competent when it came to schemes, but naive to the finer points of program-building. As I began to explore different ways to improve as a head coach, I embarked on the journey of researching some of the top high school football teams across the country with the purpose of gaining insight into these coaches and programs. It seemed obvious to me that if I wanted to build an elite program, there could be no better teachers than those who have gone before me and accomplished just that.

As I began my research, I set out to compare and contrast high school football in my home state of Washington with programs around the country. During this process, it occurred to me that there would be many others who could benefit from the findings I was about to uncover. It was with these aspirations that I set out to begin this tour of some of the top football programs. Initially, the three things I set out to accomplish were: determining common factors amongst elite programs, identifying unique approaches to the game of high school football, and examining high school football across ten states through the lenses of twelve of the most successful programs in the country. I would credit my invested time as a success if I were to accomplish these three goals. Fortunately, not only was I able to meet these goals, but I was also able to experience some unanticipated moments that enriched my experience.

My research began with studying the *USA Today* final rankings for high school football over the past ten seasons. Because the *USA Today* rankings are often known to be the national measuring stick for high school football, it was a natural starting place for my research. I elected a short time span of ten years since I'm a firm believer that high school football evolves. What might have proven to be a successful program in the 1980s or 1990s, would likely fall short if implemented as one of today's programs.

During this analytical first step of my research, many schools jumped out at me. When determining what programs I wanted to pursue, I realized that I could broaden my research by selecting programs spanning numerous states. This process resulted in the selection of twelve programs located in ten states; the two states providing two schools were Texas and Florida. Going into this project, I was certain that I wanted to draw knowledge from: Texas, Florida, California, Ohio, Pennsylvania, and Georgia—the rest were wildcards.

South Panola High School, located in Mississippi, wrapped up their 2007 season with the longest current winning streak in the nation; they were victorious at seventy-five straight games—they became a clear choice. Charlotte Independence, located in North Carolina, recently maintained a 109 game winning streak that was snapped during the 2007 season; they were added to the list. Then Jenks High School, located in Oklahoma, had just won their ninth 6A state championship in twelve years; they made the cut. Finally, I had to choose between two stellar programs located in Louisiana. It became evident that John Curtis Christian High School and Evangel Christian Academy were very similar in their successes, making the selection a very difficult one. Because a recent book was written about John Curtis, I chose to write about Evangel instead.

The twelve schools selected hold an impressive combined record of 627-54-2 over the past four years; they also have thirty state championships amongst them in the past four years. Initially, there were many things that I wanted to compare and contrast regarding these phenomenal programs. I set out to understand: the strength and conditioning programs, the coaching staff sizes, the amount of money paid to each coaching staff, the amount of power each high school coach exercises over their feeder programs, the quality and type of facilities at each school, the Division One talent sent forth, the roles of booster clubs to the programs, the importance of youth football to the high school programs, and whether race seemed to play into the success of these schools.

Aside from these general areas, I wanted to take a closer look at the offensive and defensive systems that each program used; I also wanted to evaluate how many of the programs had players play on both offense and defense. Another exploration that interested me was if and how each team trained players during athletic periods. Then, there were comparisons to be made about the head coaches themselves. How old were the head coaches of these top national programs? Did longevity, or new coaches contribute to their successes? And, how did the head coaches' work days compare/contrast with each another?

Of course, I could have written a book about twenty schools instead of twelve, but that didn't feel right. I knew that if I were to conduct a thorough job on this research, I would compromise the quality of my findings if the book became too cumbersome. I do not claim, by any means, that the schools I have chosen are the top twelve programs in the country; I do believe, however, that each one epitomizes facets of unquestionable success. They have all proven that they deserve to be titled Gridiron Dynasties.

PART I

Colerain High School

Cincinnati, Ohio

Overview

EVEN BEFORE THE movie *We Are Marshall*, the Colerain faithful would break out in, "We are Colerain" chants during their football games. To the Colerain Cardinals, this ritual is much more than a trendy chant, but rather a proclamation of unity. As Head Coach Tom Bolden states, "Colerain football is who we are; it is not what we do but rather who we are."

Colerain football is a well-oiled machine that runs an unbelievable strength and conditioning program. This football program not only develops the football players who are currently attending Colerain High School, but buses in between fifty-five and ninety seventh and eighth graders for training as well. The goal is to give the middle school players a head start on the competition that they will be up against a few years down the road. In order to not conflict with other sports, this training does not begin until after the middle school basketball season is finished. It is unique to have a program that incorporates the future Cardinals in such a way that they can be trained by the Colerain High School football coaches before they even get to the high school.

Students who are attending Colerain, or are on the path to Colerain, seem to have little problem with the strong commitment it takes to be part of this team—the results come with it. Since 2000, Colerain Football has achieved a record of 97-9. The players, parents, coaches, and community recognize that this caliber of success comes at a price.

During the off-season, Cardinal football players train every Monday, Tuesday, Thursday, and Friday. The only day that the team takes off from the four days per week schedule is Christmas. That is why when meeting for an interview with Coach Bolden on an early holiday morning when school was not in session, over 60 players were observed going through a grueling workout which has become synonymous with Colerain football.

One impressive illustration of how dedicated this team is comes with a sacrifice that all players make at Colerain High School—they do not drink soda pop. This is one of the team rules. In regard to this rule, Coach Bolden says, "We don't drink soda [because] it is not good for you. [It's as] simple as that."

The Strength Program

COACH BOLDEN STATES that in order to win games, "Your team must be physically superior to the team you are playing against, and if you aren't, you must find a way to get there through your strength and conditioning program." This is the reasoning behind starting strength and conditioning training while players are still in middle school, as well as having all twelve coaches present at almost every workout throughout the year.

A major reason that the weight room is such a priority at Colerain is because Coach Bolden believes he needs to compensate for the disadvantage that Ohio high schools have as a result of not holding spring football. Needless to say, when the Cardinals play an out-of-state opponent early in the season, they will have had far fewer practices than their opponent; this is where the weight room comes into play. The current weight room could be described as functional, but not glamorous, and it stands at roughly twenty-five hundred square feet. Coach Bolden has plans to begin fundraising for a field house that would include a bigger weight room.

The Principle

WHILE MOST SCHOOLS are just striving to train their athletes, Colerain is aiming to do it with the highest level of efficiency. The coaches at Colerain structure their workouts in ways that will maximize success on the field during the season. Each off-season, the coaching staff generates a list of the 50 returning players who are projected to make the biggest impacts during the upcoming season. Each of the coaches then becomes responsible for developing four of the players during training. With a ratio of one coach to four players, these 50 players are not only closely monitored, but also held to a higher level of accountability by their coaches. It is significant to note that these coaches are not only accepting the responsibility for the physical development of these players, but are focusing on the mental development as well. These 4:1 ratios allow the coaches to push each player extremely hard during the off-season workouts—this results in superiorly-trained team members who are mentally tougher than their opponents in the fall.

The 2004 Team

WHEN APPROACHING THE main entrance to Colerain High School, there is a single championship banner hanging from the 2004 season; this is the only state football championship in school history. The 2004 team finished fifth in the country according to the poll conducted by *USA Today*; this is the highest national ranking in school history. Additionally, Colerain has finished in the top twenty-five for three out of the last four years according to *USA Today*.

From the 2004 team, there were: three players who signed scholarships with the University of Michigan, four with Ohio State University, and eight with the University of Cincinnati. It is a remarkable statistic that the starting defense only allowed opponents into the end zone three times during the fifteen games in the season; the offense averaged 46.3 points per game. During the state finals, the Colerain Cardinals fumbled three of their first four possessions inside their own thirty yard line. As a result of the three turnovers, the defense only gave up three points, and then cruised to a 50-10 victory. During that same game, the starting quarterback rushed for 257 yards; it was clearly a dominating finish to a spectacular season.

One has to wonder how the 2004 team would have matched up with the most impressive teams throughout high school football history. Off the field, the 2004 team was standing out in the weight room. They had: seventeen players bench press over three hundred pounds, two players bench press over four hundred pounds, and one player bench press over five hundred pounds. Ten players squatted over five hundred pounds, six players squatted over six hundred pounds, and one squatted over seven hundred pounds. Additionally, multiple players were able to rep over three hundred pounds on the power clean. It probably won't be too long until a few of these 2004 members are seen playing football on Sundays.

The Game Weeks

WHEN THE SCHOOL bell rings at 7:40 AM each morning at Colerain High School, the football team has already been in attendance for at least forty minutes. Players arrive before 7:00 AM each morning during the season to be on time for 7:00 AM film sessions of their Friday night opponent. This also serves as a way for the coaching staff to ensure the players get to their first period classes on time. After a twenty-five minute film session, players are off to classes until school ends at 2:40 PM.

At 3:00 PM, the two and one-half hour practice starts promptly. After practice, the players then have around thirty minutes to shower and attend their second film session of the day. While the players are showering, the practice film that was just recorded is being burned onto DVDs for each of the coaches. From 6:00–7:00 PM, the players are once again broken up into groups with their position coaches to review the practice they just completed. After the twelve hour day, the coaches and players head home. They begin the same process over again the following morning.

Saturdays are no exception to the dedication of this football team. On Saturday mornings following a Friday night game, the team comes in to review the film from the previous night's game. After reviewing the game film with their position coaches, they stretch, lift, run, and receive treatments if needed. When all of the hours for school and football are totaled, each player ends up putting in a sixty-two hour week.

The Challenges

THE NORTHWEST LOCAL School District that Colerain High School is part of has not passed a levy in thirteen years. As a result, students have to pay a one hundred dollar participation fee to be part of Colerain football. Out of the twenty-two school districts in the area, Northwest Local School District ranks nineteenth in teacher pay. As for the amount of each of the coaching stipends compared with the other nine teams in Colerain's league, they have the fewest number and the lowest amount per stipend. Coach Bolden will earn around seventy-two hundred dollars in 2008; his highest paid assistants will make fifty-six hundred dollars.

Colerain could be considered a modern day *Hoosiers* when

comparing its population to their opposing teams. It is worth noting that in Colerain's ten-team league, they are the smallest school. Ironically, Colerain plays against three out of four of Ohio's largest high schools: Fairfield, Oak Hills, and Mason High School.

According to Ohio laws, public high schools have little ability to draw athletes from any population outside of their high school boundaries. For example, if a student at Northwest High School, the other high school in Colerain's district, wanted to transfer to Colerain, he would have to go through the Ohio governing body for this transfer approval—this is seldom granted. Needless to say, unless a student physically moves into Colerain boundaries, he cannot play for the athletic team.

In contrast to Colerain, the major private school powerhouses in the state of Ohio, such as St. Xavier, that has double the number of males as Colerain, can legally recruit students/players from anywhere without restrictions. While many public schools in Ohio want to see the private schools compete in separate classifications, as is the case in many other states, Coach Bolden welcomes the challenge of competing against these private schools.

Recruiting

DURING THIS PAST recruiting season, over one hundred college coaches visited Colerain High School looking for talent. As a matter of fact, on the first day of recruiting, five different Mid-American Conference coaches arrived simultaneously.

Coach Bolden has a system in place to promote his players while maintaining his busy schedule. First, he shows each of his prospects how to use Colerain's video system to create their own highlight films. Next, he explains to each player what type of plays should be included in their films. Then, he burns plenty of DVDs of each player's highlight films to have in hand when coaches come looking for talent.

When college coaches arrive at Colerain seeking talent, they leave with the DVDs of the players who interest them; they also are given transcripts and test scores. The collaborative effort between the players and Coach Bolden resulted in 13 players signing scholarships on the 2008 signing day for a total of 1.2 million dollars. To help put this in perspective, only 39 players signed scholarships from Colerain's ten-team league. One third of the scholarships given in this league went to Colerain High School—this is pretty remarkable for the smallest school in the league.

The Future Players

TWO HUNDRED-FIFTY CHILDREN aged six through eleven years old who are on track to attend Colerain High School participate in the Little Cards youth football program. This Little Cards program functions separately from the high school program, and is not financed in any way by the Colerain Booster Club. This does, however, benefit Colerain by providing youth with the chance to get involved in football at early ages, consequently connecting them to the high school. Most of these youth will look forward to playing in front of ten thousand Colerain fans at halftime during one of the home games.

As a support, Coach Bolden and his staff offer free clinics for the coaches of the Little Cards. A major difference from the coaches who coach the Little Cards and the coaches who coach most youth programs is that the Little Cards do not have any of their parents coaching the team. That is one of the rules within the program. The coaches are drawn from former players of Colerain High and other volunteers who feel the same passion for Colerain Football. Coach Bolden will occasionally make appearances at some of the games, but this youth program is thriving and developing the future Colerain High players with minimal effort from the head coach.

Ohio vs. USA Challenge

FORMER OHIO STATE quarterback, Kirk Herbstreit, has recently created the Ohio vs. USA Challenge. Started in 2005, this is quickly becoming an important event that is being used to measure how the top teams in Ohio match up with the rest of the country. Longtime recruiting analyst, Tom Lemming, has called the event, "by far, the best high school event ever staged."

The Ohio vs. USA Challenge is a terrific opportunity for Ohio high school coaches to prepare their teams for early season games; they play against out of state opponents who have practiced during spring football. Spring football is one major difference between the state of Ohio and teams from other states around the country. Because the state of Ohio does not participate in spring football, one would think that the other teams would have a significant advantage coming from states that permit spring football. In Florida, for example, players are given the opportunity to practice for twenty days in the spring *including* one official spring football game in May against another school. Yet, in spite of not having spring football, the Ohio programs have proven in the Ohio vs. USA Challenge that they match up very well against programs in the rest of the nation.

In 2005, the Ohio vs. USA Challenge featured two games; one included Colerain beating Texas Lee 27-12. In 2006, the event grew to ten games, with nine of them featuring top Ohio programs and some top-notch out of state opponents including: Lakeland (Florida), De La Salle (California), Don Bosco Prep (New Jersey.), and Byrnes (South Carolina).

In 2007, the event expanded in such a way that six national powerhouses were matched against one another. One of these games featured St. Xavier (Ohio) against Dematha (Maryland). These two programs came into the 2007 game ranked fourth and fifth in the nation, according to *USA Today*. At the game, St. Xavier defeated Dematha 28-7. The second game faced off Elder High

School (Ohio) with Independence High School (North Carolina). With 109 consecutive games won, Independence arrived with the longest winning streak in the nation; Elder (Ohio) defeated Independence (North Carolina) 41-34 and snapped their impressive winning streak. The last featured game was a showdown between Colerain (Ohio) and Hoover (Alabama); Colerain walked away with a 20-17 win. Other out of state teams that competed in 2007 included: Pittsburgh Central Catholic (Pennsylvania), Long Beach Poly (California) and Union High School (Oklahoma).

High School Football in Ohio

THERE ARE A few things that make Ohio's high school football distinctive. First, the high school playoff bracket is set up by splitting the state up into four separate regions; the top eight teams from each region or area makeup one-quarter of the playoff bracket. By developing brackets this way, it is ensured that only one team from each region will advance to the state semi-finals each year. Region Four, where Colerain competes, is considered to be the best region in the state.

Next, it is worth looking at how the top eight teams from each region are selected. Through a high-tech computerized system, these teams are ranked and eventually seeded into the playoff bracket (these can be seen at www.joeeitel.com). Then, the computer system determines which teams will have home-field advantages in the first round of the playoffs. After the first round, each game is played on a neutral field, frequently drawing very large crowds. An illustration of this was in 2001 when Colerain played Elder High School in a playoff game in front of forty-two thousand people at Paul Brown Stadium.

Finally, the tradition that contributes to Ohio's uniqueness is the Division One Championship. Around one hundred-twenty schools from Ohio compete each year for this championship—high school football's biggest prize in Ohio. It is remarkable to note that Colerain's region, Region Four, has produced the state champion each of the last seven years.

Lowndes High School

Valdosta, Georgia

Overview

LOWNDES HIGH SCHOOL, located in Valdosta Georgia, has an original way to gauge how well they are performing during games—fans contribute loud cheers when their players are playing well and hostile boos when they are playing poorly. It seems that most of the Lowndes faithful have an above-average grasp of the game of football. The one hundred-forty page football program serves to inform the fans of the different facets of the Lowndes football program—it also adds to the experience of Friday nights. In recent history, there have been more cheers than boos; the team claimed three of the last four Georgia High School 5A state championships. Outside of the stands, fans are also very loyal supporters of their team as well—this was evidenced by the six thousand faithful who lined the streets in celebration of the 2007 state championship on a forty degree, rainy day.

The fans in the stands are not the only ones who reinforce the good and the bad performances of the team. A local restaurant, Sonny's BBQ, caters the team's pre-game meal each week free of charge the week following a victory. In 2007, Sonny's BBQ contributed over fifteen hundred pre-game meals—on the house—as a result of fourteen wins produced by the Vikings. The sheer size of the Lowndes band, three hundred-seventy members strong, also illustrates the support of the Lowndes Vikings. The immensity of this band required fifteen buses to transport them to the Georgia Dome for the state title game in 2007. At home games, the Lowndes band is frequently given warnings by referees for being too loud throughout a contest. One of the most spectacular displays of fan support comes with the notorious Lowndes vs. Valdosta rivalry. Some would say this is one of the nation's finest rivalries within one of the top leagues in the nation.

The Rivalry

WHEN LOWNDES HIGH school was established at its current location in the 1960's, there wasn't a strong rivalry between them and perennial national power Valdosta High School. While the players from Valdosta would play Lowndes, they knew they would face a team composed of primarily country kids; a team who would play hard but wouldn't win the game. Though only five miles apart geographically, Lowndes and Valdosta were worlds apart in their abilities. It was during this era when such extreme differences were seen between the schools that Valdosta, being the city school, nicknamed the Lowndes Vikings the "Plow Boys".

Hiram Johnson, one of Lowndes' coaches since 1973, says that the Lowndes community eventually began to take pride in the "Plow Boys" nickname, making it a well-known symbol of pride for today's Lowndes community. Straw hats and overalls, the work attire of farmers, began to symbolize the workmanlike attitude of the people of Lowndes. In January of 1976, at the annual game between Lowndes and Valdosta, a rivalry was born. Joe Wilson, the offensive coordinator for Valdosta, had left his school nine months earlier to become the Head Coach of Lowndes. After nine months with Head Coach Wilson, the Vikings knocked off Valdosta for the first time in school history. Joe Wilson had defeated his previous boss, and fans of Lowndes then showered the streets with hay in triumphant joy over the victory.

Today, the game between Valdosta and Lowndes is huge to both programs. Valdosta, one of the most successful programs in high school football history (with twenty-three state championships and six national championships to their name) now looks to Lowndes as the team to knock off. Valdosta leads the overall series with Lowndes 33-13; Lowndes has won the most recent four games. The Viking's current head coach, Randy McPherson, says, "By living in Lowndes, and being part of this [rivalry] game, you think of it every day of the year in some way or another."

One unique facet of the Lowndes vs. Valdosta rivalry comes in the form of not being mean-spirited. Players from opposing teams know each other from playing youth football together. It is not uncommon for relatives to be sitting on opposite sides of the bleachers. Sometimes brothers and sisters attend rival schools. Having families split between the two schools comes from the way that Georgia structures their servicing areas. In this educational service area of the city of Valdosta, a student leaving eighth grade is given the option of choosing to go to Lowndes or Valdosta. Once he/she declares a school, he/she is unable to change schools without athletic ramifications. Currently, Lowndes is running at full capacity, making it rare for the school to accept students from outside their school's boundaries; this is in spite of Georgia's rule allowing for a one-time move.

The Lowndes vs. Valdosta games are always sold out regardless of which team is hosting the contest. The game, which often times has a region championship on the line, is the hottest ticket in town. When this game is hosted by Lowndes, the booster club the first opportunities to buy tickets. Fans camp out overnight to have the first crack at the roughly three hundred remaining tickets. When the game is hosted at Valdosta, Coach McPherson says it is everything he can do to get two tickets per player just for his athletes' parents to be able to watch the game.

It goes without saying that players feel the magnitude of the game as well. Coaches find themselves having to calm players down so that they do not try to over-perform in the game, but keep their attention on their specified assignments. At a recent contest between the two schools, the Lowndes kicker actually hyperventilated from the pressure of the game; he was able to return in the second half. All who are privileged enough to attend experience the intense pressure of this Valdosta vs. Lowndes rivalry.

The League

THE EIGHT-TEAM LEAGUE/REGION that Lowndes plays in is comparable to the Southeastern Conference of college football. Like the Southeastern Conference, Lowndes' league/region is arguably the best league in all of high school football. In Georgia, the eight teams that compete against each other annually are referred to as a region, rather than a league. Tim Cokely, the former Head Coach at Colquitt County High School, one of the members of Lowndes' region, described the region to the Valdosta Daily Times as one of the toughest regions in the country. The head coach of Warner Robins told the Valdosta Daily Times that, "It's like a playoff atmosphere every week." Other coaches in the region also portray their schedules week in and week out as being similar to playing playoff teams every week of the year.

The teams that make up Lowndes' region include: Warner Robins, Northside Warner Robins, Houston County, Coffee, Tift, Valdosta, Lowndes, and Colquitt County. Each school has its own impressive résumé, thus keeping good teams out of the playoffs each year. Warner Robin holds four state titles with their most recent being a 4A title in 2004. In total, they have won twenty-three region championships and two national championships. Northside Warner Robins joined the region in 2008. They bring a 44-1 record over the past three seasons; this includes back to back undefeated seasons claiming two 4A state titles along the way. Northside Warner Robins' only loss in the last three years was a three-point defeat in the 2005 state finals.

Houston County beat Lowndes at home in 2006 and has been to the playoffs three of the past four years; Kyle Moore, the starting defensive end for the University of Southern California came from their program. Coffee High School won the region championship in 2002 and has made the playoffs five out of the past six years. Tift High School was a state semi-finalist and regional champion in 2006; they were also a state runner-up in 1997, and won a state championship in 1983. Valdosta high school holds twenty-three state championships, as well as six national championships—two of which were according to USA Today in 1984 and 1986. Lowndes has won the 5A state championship three of the past four years. Lastly, Colquitt County hired former Hoover High School (Alabama) coach Rush Probst to make his debut in the fall of 2008. Probst went 115-11 while at Hoover High School, and won the Alabama 6A state championships in 1998, 2000, 2002, 2003, and 2004.

This phenomenal region has been set apart by the great fortune of having very good coaches throughout its history. In 2007, Head Coach Randy McPherson of Lowndes held the position of the senior member of the region entering his sixth year at Lowndes. Former Hoover Head Coach Rush Probst recently replaced legendary Florida high school coach Tim Cokely. Cokely came to Colquitt from North Florida Christian where he had a 107-24 record and five state championships from 1996-2004. Cokely left Colquitt with a record of 5-17 in region play. Cokely today stands as one example of a highly successful coach elsewhere who clearly struggled in what is arguably the toughest region, or league, in the nation.

The Team Leadership

LEADERSHIP WITHIN A high school football team is often a major predictor of how far a team advances in its season. Developing leadership within his program is a top priority for Coach McPherson; he holds a unique philosophy on how to best foster this leadership. In the off-season, the Viking's team is randomly split into groups of six athletes. Each member of the team is then graded weekly in four areas: attendance, discipline (staying out of trouble), grades, and community service. The results of these assessments are posted in the locker room for all to see.

An example of how this system works is as follows: players may lose five points for every F they have on a grade check, yet they receive positive points for A's and B's. If an athlete takes part in some form of community service, he will earn positive points as well. It is interesting to note that church attendance is counted as one way of getting community service points. Each month, the team with the highest combined score gets to eat at Outback Steakhouse with Coach McPherson and order anything on the menu—free of charge. Through this system, players have opportunities to learn leadership through the act of holding their teammates accountable and encouraging them to make positive choices. It is commendable that Coach McPherson doesn't merely talk of the role of leadership, but rather offers venues for players to develop this character trait during the off-season.

Another way that Lowndes players strive toward stronger leadership is through the participation of character lessons before practices; this takes place once a week. In a ten- minute increment, one of the Viking's coaches leads the team through a lesson out of the book titled *Coaching to Change Lives,* by Dennis Parker and D.W. Rutledge. Additionally, every Wednesday before practice, the team takes part in a Christian devotional. In the summer before the 2007 season, the entire Lowndes team attended a Fellowship of Christian Athletes (FCA) camp together. At the FCA camp, they not only competed in seven on seven competitions, but participated in team-building activities together. According to McPherson, the FCA camp was a positive experience and served as a way to bring his team close together.

The Facilities

LOWNDES' OWN MARTIN Stadium has a seating capacity of thirteen thousand. A current project to improve multiple facilities is scheduled to be completed by the fall of 2008. Part of the project includes adding one thousand end zone seats to bring the total capacity to fourteen thousand; they will also remove grass and replace it with field turf. Uniquely, there is no track around the football stadium—this is a positive attribute to the football atmosphere. Part of the upcoming renovation includes the addition of two locker rooms in one of the end zones.

Currently located in one of the end zones is a football field house which houses: the weight room, a coach's office, locker room, and equipment room. By the fall of 2008, the Vikings will own a brand new fifty-two hundred square foot weight room equipped with twenty-four Power Rack stations. The current weight room will eventually become a meeting room for the team; it will be divided into two rooms for offensive and defensive meetings to take place simultaneously. Presently, the team uses two practice fields in addition to the new field-turf game field. The baseball team is housed in a separate field house with an indoor hitting cage and weight room designed strictly for their use. In addition to these facilities, the completion of an 8 million dollar gymnasium was just completed. It is amazing that the elaborate facilities at Lowndes are strikingly comparable to the other teams in their region.

The Program

LOWNDES FOLLOWS THE Bigger, Faster, Stronger workout program where teams lift weights on Mondays, Wednesdays, and Fridays. They utilize this both in season and out of season. The Vikings players perform box squats and towel bench press as part of their Friday workouts on game days. The towel bench press is an exercise where the athlete places a rolled up towel on his chest while bench pressing; this exercise primarily works the triceps. In addition, the box squat isolates the workload to the quadriceps and does not utilize much of the hamstrings. With these two exercises, the coaches believe that they can gain from lifting workouts on game days while maintaining their Monday, Wednesday, and Friday lifting schedules.

Members of the football team are required to participate in one weight lifting class each semester. There are four sections of the class offered each semester with three coaches teaching the classes. With this approach, there are at least two coaches who team teach the class. Baseball also has two sections of weight lifting in the baseball field house for a combined total of ten sections of weight lifting over the school year.

The number one indicator of the Vikings' team strength is the power clean. Coach McPherson doesn't make a big deal about the bench press because it takes care of itself with all the players focusing on strong bench presses. The coaches instead focus their efforts on the power clean and squat. As a result, the 2007 team included fifty-nine players who each power cleaned two hundred twenty-five pounds or more. The 2008 team is projected to have at least ten players with a power clean of at least three hundred pounds. The strength and conditioning program at Lowndes High School is a huge factor in having achieved three state championships over the past four seasons.

The Coaching Staff

AFTER THE 2001 season, Lowndes High School was seeking a new head football coach. With one hour left until the collection of job applications officially closed, Randy McPherson called the assistant superintendent of Lowndes School District to see if the committee already had a person in mind or if the job were truly open. The answer that came back was that the job was wide open. McPherson then faxed in his résumé within the hour to meet the deadline. He wasn't the committee's first choice; McPherson was the second-choice candidate initially. Sometimes, the second choice ends up being better than the first. After the committee's first choice decided not to take the job McPherson then accepted it. McPherson said that when he was a high school player, he didn't know he was going to go to college until his high school coach told him he was going to go to college. McPherson doubts he would have gone to college and become a head coach if it weren't for the motivation supplied by his own high school football coach.

Currently, Coach McPherson maintains an entire staff of eighteen coaches. Ten out of thirteen varsity/junior varsity coaches are paid positions, and three are volunteers. The ninth grade program also has five paid coaches. All fifteen paid coaches work in the high school building. Along with being the head coach, McPherson is the county athletic director, a job that has him overseeing all of the high school athletic programs and both of the middle school programs. The other fourteen coaches on his staff teach three out of four periods at Lowndes High School. Out of those coaches, three coaches teach only weight lifting classes.

Both middle schools run the same offensive and defensive systems as the high school and follow the same weight-training program. Players become part of the Lowndes program in the sixth grade, through a club team, prior to feeding into the middle schools. Harmony resounds amongst the coaches who compose this complex football program. The result of this is ownership within the program, coupled with a very small turnover in coaches, both contributing to the program's success.

To help build their program, the staff also runs a separate spring practice session for the incoming freshmen. Georgia rules allow for each team to hold ten days of spring practice. Lowndes holds ten days of spring football in February, and then they bring in the incoming freshmen separately in April for ten days with the entire coaching staff. This allows the incoming players more individualized coaching and smoother transitions into the high school program.

The Coaching Philosophy

LOWNDES DIFFERS FROM the other schools in that its coaching staff is split offensively and defensively, but their players are not. Coach McPherson attributes this philosophy to the tactic of putting the best players on defense. Many schools claim that they implement this strategy, but Lowndes does it completely. Coach McPherson says that teams who don't have their players practice both sides of the ball and really do put their best players all on defense will have a tough time scoring, or for that matter, even moving the ball at times. As a result, Lowndes can use very talented defensive players on offense when necessary to move the ball.

A Lowndes practice in August would show a team going live to the ground with a whistle. In spring practices they also go live to the ground, without a whistle. This physical brand of football translates to a physical product on Friday nights. As for the reviewing of filmed games with the team, each coach leaves Friday night games with a copy of the film. Each coach grades the performances of the players he coaches. The coaching staff then gathers on Sunday afternoon to prepare for their next opponent. On Mondays, the team watches selected clips from the previous game for no more than fifteen minutes prior to hitting the field in preparation for their next opponent. On Tuesday in class, the three coaches who work in the weight room, along with Coach McPherson; all review the entire film of the previous game with every member of the team.

On game days, the coaching staff keeps the athletes with them from the end of school until kickoff. After school, they usually share in a pre-game meal, hopefully catered for free as a result of their previous win. Then, they head to the gym for a walk-through. Next, they head to the wrestling room to relax and watch a movie until they go to the stadium.

The Funding

IN 2007, LOWNDES ticket sales profited the school over $460,000. It is in part because of this revenue that the football program is granted a healthy $175,000 annual budget. The amount of money paid to football coaches for coaching supplements each year at Lowndes totals $150,820. At both middle schools, which feed directly into Lowndes High School, $18,750 is granted each year to football coaches for the purpose of coaching supplements.

The booster club serving the Viking's football program is vibrant as well. The booster club generates around $150,000 annually to assist in funding the program. Presently, there are over twelve hundred members in the booster club—they all pay dues each year to be part of it. Observably, this not only benefits the football program, but also ensures that participants are given opportunities to purchase tickets to popular contests. Two golf tournaments, the sales of football merchandise, and the dues paid by the booster club members make up the bulk of the $150,000 raised annually for the program.

Recruiting

LOWNDES FOOTBALL DOESN'T contribute as many athletes to Division One Schools as their team's success would suggest. In

2004, Lowndes sent three players to Division One schools; this was the most in their history up to this point. In 2005, the team had twelve kids sign with Division 1AA schools and Division Two schools, but none at Division 1A level. NFL linebacker Randall Godfrey, and NFL defensive lineman Jay Ratliff, both hail from Lowndes High School.

Evangel Christian Academy

Shreveport, Louisiana

Overview

EVANGEL CHRISTIAN ACADEMY, located in Shreveport, Louisiana, has won seven football state championships in the past ten years. Alumni John David Booty (USC), Jacob Hester (LSU), and Brock Berlin (University of Florida), all brought the school and football program tremendous notoriety. It could be argued, however, that it was Josh David Booty who put the Evangel Eagles on the map. Josh David Booty, the older brother of former USC quarterback John David Booty, came out of high school ranked higher than Peyton Manning as a quarterback.

The enrollment of this small private school, affiliated with Shreveport Community Church, has recently declined in part because of the opening of Calvary Baptist Academy, a school founded by the Booty family. Presently, Evangel has an enrollment of six hundred-fifty students grades K-12; two hundred-fifty of those span grades nine through twelve. In 1999, Evangel finished first in the nation according to five out of eight polls, and second in the nation as reported by the *USA Today* poll. One year earlier, in 1998, the Eagles had finished third according to the *USA Today* poll.

One ingredient leading to the accomplishments of the Evangel football program is the implementation of the theory that in order to improve, a team must play against the toughest competition it can schedule. During a sixty game winning streak, Evangel traveled from Louisiana to Texas multiple times, making stops in other states as well, to play against programs that would raise their level of performance. Miraculously, during a 60-0 run in recent history, the Evangel Eagles didn't have one varsity starter miss a start along the way.

Current Chancellor Denny Duron, whose parents founded Evangel Christian Academy, shares his parents' broad vision for Evangel. This is evident when viewing the school's campus and stadium. While many other private schools have to sacrifice a home field advantage and rent stadiums from other schools, Evangel owns their own stadium. Yet, with tuition for the private school around five thousand dollars per year Evangel doesn't have a lot of funding for their program. When the stadium was expanded, current Chancellor Denny Duron went on faith that the needed funds would be raised. Evangel actually purchased the expansion prior to even raising a cent. Presently, the Eagle's team has three and a-half practice fields for the sixty player varsity team; there is also allotted room for expansion. One of the end zones has a cement slab situated to become the home of new locker rooms. Plans are also underway for a new weight room with a capacity to train one hundred athletes at a time. The high school, which was added to the K-8 school in 1989, has quickly risen from a rookie program to one with an impressive record that includes multiple state championships. It goes without saying that the Evangel Eagles anticipate many more successes to come.

The Beginning

CURRENT CHANCELLOR DENNY Duron once played quarterback for Louisiana Tech and won two 1AA National Championships. After finishing his college career, he was drafted into the World Football League as a quarterback, and led his team to the World Football League Championship. He then had a shot at the National Football League (NFL) with the Washington Redskins. At this crossroad, Duron felt that he was called into Christian ministry; this resulted in him turning down a chance at the NFL to focus on his calling.

When Duron arrived at Evangel, he envisioned an institution that would resemble a public school in look, but would be grounded in a Christian worldview. With a heart for the inner-city, it is not surprising that a very diverse student population composes the small private Christian school in Shreveport, Louisiana. It is estimated that roughly fifty percent of the student population at Evangel is Caucasian.

In 1989, Evangel, which had just added grades 9-12 to the K-8 school, began playing football. It certainly wasn't a glamorous start to the now storied program. Denny Duron was the first coach of the rookie football team. Evangel's humble start included acquiring donated equipment from other programs as a result of limited financial resources. The equipment they received from other schools was ten to twelve years old and on the verge of being discarded.

At the program's debut, the program started its first year with only fifteen players, and fourteen of them had no high school football experience. In the beginning, Evangel's goal was to simply provide the attending students with the opportunity to play football. Nobody, including the original coaches and players, could have anticipated that in the first eighteen years of the program's existence, the program would win ten state championships and produce two *USA Today* offensive players of the year.

The Cornerstone Principle

DEEPLY IMBEDDED IN the Evangel formula of success is the cornerstone principle that a team must go against the toughest competition it can schedule in order to improve the most. Current Head Coach John Bachman attributes this philosophy to Chancellor and former Head Coach, Denny Duron, who is currently serving as an assistant coach. By way of putting this belief into action, Evangel is the national program that takes its show on the road more than any other school of its caliber. Head Coach John Bachman is up front with the reality that Evangel sometimes learns tough lessons from the difficult opponents they face. It is through these difficulties, however, that Evangel is granted opportunities for progression.

Many of the quality opponents that Evangel plays are located outside of Louisiana. Evangel has played perennial Texas power Lufkin High School on three occasions, winning twice and losing once. One of the more memorable victories in Evangel history includes a 2001 victory against Lufkin. In that game, Lufkin came in ranked 4th in the nation—for good reason. It was, after all, future Texas A&M and NFL quarterback Reggie McNeal's senior season at Lufkin. After the loss to Evangel in 2001, Lufkin went on to win their remaining games—they then claimed the 5A State Title in Texas.

Another memorable victory was against Dallas Carter (Texas) that had eighteen Division 1A players on their team that year. Included in their traveling game schedule, Evangel also played Marshall and Carroll High Schools, both of Texas. In 2006, traveling to Southlake, Texas to play Carroll High School provided Evangel with a defeat where Evangel gained valuable lessons. In 2008, Evangel is ready to travel to defending 4A state champion, Lake Travis High School, in Austin, Texas— another attempt to tackle one of the top Texas programs.

One of the supreme examples of how aggressively Evangel

schedules opponents came in 2003 when Evangel visited Missouri to play Rock Hurst High School in a Saturday night showdown. Rock Hurst was led by senior Tony Temple; he went on to become a standout running back at the University of Missouri. After defeating Rock Hurst, Evangel headed to Alabama to play perennial Alabama powerhouse Hoover High School on a Thursday. With just five days between the games, Evangel only squeezed in two days of practice before playing Hoover. It was at the game with Hoover where Evangel was badly defeated—this provided the valuable lesson of how difficult it is to come into a game and play at 100% with limited practice time. As if out of state contests against Rock Hurst and Hoover weren't enough, Evangel also traveled to play the number one ranked team in the nation, and the eventual *USA Today* national champion of 2003, De La Salle High School of Concord, California. At this game, De La Salle defeated Evangel. It is worth noting that the Evangel coaching staff praised both the De La Salle team and their Head Coach, Bob Ladouceur, for both the excellence of their program and the high level of class De La Salle showed in their victory.

Throughout recent years, Evangel has played: Springdale (Arkansas) three times, Cretin-Derham Hall (St. Paul, Minnesota), Suwannee High School (Florida), and multiple top programs from Mississippi as well. Evangel also schedules the best from their own state, Louisiana, as well. The ten contests between Evangel and Louisiana powerhouse, West Monroe High School, exemplify the best of their home state competition. As of late, however, Evangel is finding it more difficult get the top Louisiana programs scheduled in the regular season. With a rise to national stardom coming upon Evangel in such a short period of time, one can conclude that the current Chancellor Denny Duron's belief in playing the toughest competition possible has certainly been a key ingredient to the Evangel football success.

The Atmosphere

THE ATMOSPHERE OF the Evangel Christian Academy campus is different from most any other school. When players and coaches come and go from one another, they tell each other that they love them. Coaches also admit that they are not afraid to cry with their players or pray with them. Head Coach John Bachman makes it clear in his softly-spoken, humble demeanor that the goal of Evangel is to arm kids for life by teaching them about Jesus.

Coach Bachman says that Evangel tells athletes that football is important to God because it is important to them. One of the traditions that Evangel football upholds consists of a dedicated chapel service the night before Evangel plays in a state championship game. At this chapel service, the seniors are given the opportunity to speak. Bachman says he looks forward to what the seniors have to say. He also adds that this ritual creates a memorable experience for the team. It is worth mentioning that very few of the words spoken by the seniors pertain to football and the upcoming game. The primary focus of their messages generally includes depicting the impact that Evangel has had on their lives. An example of the type of impact Evangel coaches have on their players is illustrated in a quote by former Evangel quarterback Brock Berlin (University of Miami, University of Florida) when he told *American Monthly Football* in October of 2002, "Evangel has the best coaches in the world, they don't just care about an athlete's ability, they genuinely care about the athlete. They are like fathers to all of the players they coach. I love them all and I simply can't get enough of them."

The Program

COMPARED WITH OTHER top programs nationwide, the Evangel Eagles could be viewed as having a disadvantage when it comes to numbers. While Katy High School, of Katy, Texas, has close to three hundred-fifty players in their ninth through twelfth grade program, and Carroll High School of Southlake, Texas has over four hundred players in their ninth through twelfth grade program, Evangel offers a sharp contrast with only sixty ninth through twelfth grade players in their program. Evangel only recently added football at the seventh and eighth grade levels, adding another fifty players. Even with this addition, Evangel's roster size is diminutive in comparison to the other powerhouse programs they compete against.

Athletes at Evangel understand the payoffs of hard work. With football becoming a twelve month per year commitment, the Evangel players only get one week off in the summer, along with other normal holidays that the rest of the school enjoys. The majority of the hard work of the Eagle athletes is produced during the athletic period that the team takes part of first thing each morning. During the summer months, the team has nearly ninety percent participation during their workouts. With the Hang Clean being the number one indicator of physical strength for the Evangel coaching staff, the Eagles had over twenty players from the 2001 team who could hang clean two hundred twenty-five pounds or more. Additionally, the 2001 team had over fifteen players who could bench press three hundred pounds or more.

Evangel resembles a college football program in that they have both an academic advisor and a compliance coordinator. The academic advisor is a former teacher who aids in arranging tutors for all athletes in need of extra help. The compliance coordinator does not coach, but is responsible for ensuring that the program is in compliance with all of the state rules. Because it is difficult for all of the coaches to keep up with the changing rules governing athletics, it is beneficial for all coaches to have someone on campus overseeing this facet of high school athletics.

The Innovative Offense

FOR THOSE WHO love the game of football, watching Evangel Christian Academy play is quite an opportunity. In the 1990's, when passing teams were considered soft, the Evangel program was definitely ahead of the curve when it came to throwing the football; from the beginning, they were throwing in order to set up the run.

Up until recent history, the Evangel Eagles have generally operated out of the shotgun. However, many first-time observers would be surprised to see that the quarterback was not four to five yards deep, as in a traditional shotgun, but rather nine yards deep. This helped to negate some very good pass rushers. An example of this came when they played Dallas Carter in recent history. At times, the offensive tackles for Evangel couldn't even get a hand on the quick athletic defensive ends of Dallas Carter. The ends would come hard off of the edge and beat the offensive tackles—before they could get to the quarterback, the ball would be gone. Play after play, the defensive ends would run fifteen-yard sprints trying to get to the quarterback; play after play, they wouldn't be able to even touch the quarterback, let alone sack him. Obviously, this resulted in frustrated defensive linemen, and bewildered rival coaches who couldn't stop the potent passing attack. To execute this offense, the center was a big key. Early on, when Evangel was *spreading it and throwing it*, the center was fair game. He would have to deliver a perfect snap and then get blasted right after snapping the football. Today, Evangel varies the depth of the quarterback in the shotgun between five, seven, and nine yards deep.

One of the main philosophies of Evangel's powerful air attack is matching their best route runner against their opponent's best cover player. Evangel believes that by teaching the fundamentals of route running, including separation, they will win this matchup much more often than not, regardless of the capabilities of the opposing team's best cover guy. When Evangel does lose this match-up, they simply tip their hats to their opponent and move on.

With a much smaller coaching staff than traditional programs, it is apparent that Evangel has had sensational football minds coaching their kids from the very beginning. These coaches work with the players whenever they can. Consequently, Evangel opponents compete against a very innovative and sophisticated offense that is executed by players who are marvelous in the fundamentals of football.

Recruiting

EVANGEL CHRISTIAN ACADEMY not only prepares kids for life but also prepares a large number of them for college football and the NFL. To understand this, one can simply look at their 2001 team. This team had eighteen players go forth to sign Division One scholarships; nine of these players were seniors from that team. These nine players from Evangel compiled the highest number of Division One scholarships granted to any school during that year nationwide.

During the 2007 NFL draft, Evangel was tied with one other school for the number of rookies who were going into the NFL from their program—four. The number could easily be counted as five if first-year player Brock Berlin were included in that total. In 2008, marquee players Jacob Hester (LSU), and John David Booty (USC), were also drafted into the NFL—both played together at Evangel.

High School Football in Louisiana

FROM 1999 TO 2004, Evangel won four out of six 5A (large classification) state championships in Louisiana. Over the same period, John Curtis High School, in River Ridge, Louisiana, which mirrors Evangel High School in faith, sports, and program-building, won four out of six 4A state championships. After the 2004 season, a rule came down that forced schools to play within their own classifications according to their student populations. As a result, private schools, such as Evangel and John Curtis, could no longer opt up to higher levels. A few years after that decision was made, a new proposal came forth. If passed, this proposition will allow schools to opt up to the highest classification if they choose to, beginning in 2009.

In Louisiana, state rules permit schools to use athletic periods during the school day. It is a rule, however, that all football must be completed by the end of the school day during the off-season. In addition, schools are allowed up to fifteen days of spring football with one of the fifteen days permitted to be competition against another school. In August, programs in Louisiana are additionally permitted to participate in one scrimmage against another school and then hold a jamboree the following week, prior to the first game of the season.

Unlike the states of Ohio or Pennsylvania, private schools in Louisiana cannot have students play any competition, be it junior varsity or varsity, for one calendar year if they come from outside of the private school's servicing area. By contrast, in Ohio and Pennsylvania, for example, students can come from long distances if they want to attend a private school and be immediately eligible for competition. Stricter transfer rules apply to private schools in the state of Louisiana to discourage recruiting.

De La Salle High School

Concord, California

Overview

NO NAME IS more synonymous with high school football than De La Salle. This private Catholic school, located in Concord, California, is the measuring stick for all other high school football programs. Beginning in 1992, and stretching until 2004, De La Salle pulled off the longest consecutive game winning streak in high school football history—possibly all of sports history. The De La Salle Spartans won an unbelievable 151 consecutive games.

Throughout the process of building the winning streak, and earning championship after championship, De La Salle attracted large crowds everywhere they put the streak on the line. In 2002, they traveled to Hawaii to play a perennial Hawaii powerhouse, St. Louis High School, in front of over thirty thousand fans who were hoping to see the hometown favorite end the streak. Twelve years after the start of the unparalleled winning streak, it finally came to an end. At the beginning of the 2004 season, at Quest Field (home of the Seattle Seahawks), Bellevue High School, of Bellevue, Washington, defeated the De La Salle Spartans.

De La Salle is a private all-male school with just over one thousand students; tuition costs around twelve thousand dollars per year. For such an impeccable record, the facilities at De La Salle would not generally be considered as overly impressive—they could actually be disappointing to people who visit the prestigious program. What is notable to the Spartans' success is their consistency and longevity of leadership. Head Coach Bob Ladouceur will begin his thirtieth season as the head coach in the fall of 2008. Additionally, Terry Eidson, who has coached alongside Ladouceur for all but one of the last twenty-nine years, has served the past twenty years as the team's defensive coordinator.

Maurice Jones-Drew, running back of the Jacksonville Jaguars, and Amoni Toomer, wide receiver for the 2008 Super Bowl Champion New York Giants, are two of the most identified players to come through the program. Surprisingly, the school only contributes around one or two Division One players each year. The largest Division One signing class was in 2003 when four players went on to sign Division One scholarships. There have also been years when no Division One players came from De La Salle.

With around one hundred-eighty players in the ninth through twelfth grade program, De La Salle has finished in the top twenty-five in the nation for nine out of the last ten years according to *USA Today*. The next closest team nationwide has finished in the top twenty-five only six times. According to *USA Today*, the Spartans have concluded their seasons ranked as the very best team in America for five out of the last ten years; an additional two of these years earned them third place finishes. With the level of success this program has attained, it is apparent that De La Salle encompasses a matchless approach to building an unbeatable program.

The Program

IN 1992, HEAD Coach Bob Ladouceur grew concerned when examining the bottom tier players on his varsity team. He recognized that at some point, these athletes would realize that they were going to be third or fourth string players only to check themselves out, while not turning in their pads. These fifteen to twenty players were becoming content to just be jersey-wearers. Ladouceur observed that these players became bitter and formed their own little clique on the team; that bothered him.

To combat this problem of apathy, Ladouceur instituted commitment cards, the Spartans' name for goal cards. Each player is given one 3"x5" index card per week and is required to write three weekly goals on it: one goal is regarding the upcoming game, one goal is focused on football practice in the coming week, and one goal is directed toward the strength and conditioning for the following week. While three are just the minimum, some athletes generate five or six goals. The goals set must all be observable and measurable.

Each Friday on game days, approximately fifty-five varsity players gather for lunch and participate in the commitment card circle. At this circle, the players in rapid-fire-succession step into the center of the circle, state their names, read their goals, and then commit their goals to someone on the team; they then hand their card to the player to whom they have made their commitments.

The players are encouraged to hand the card to someone who either plays the same position, or someone who plays against that person on a regular basis. The philosophy behind this is that the person receiving the card will become responsible for watching, monitoring, and holding that person accountable during the next seven days. The following Thursday night after a team dinner, the team assimilates into groups where each player will be held accountable in front of his peers for the goals he set on the previous Friday. At this meeting, the athlete responsible for the monitoring shares his evaluation of whether or not the goals were met; this takes place in front of a small group.

As a result of implementing the commitment cards, each player is required to set attainable goals and strive to achieve them, or endure criticism from his peers. Because of the commitment card system, all players have to be engaged and focused on improvement regardless of where they stand on the depth chart; the knowledge that they will be assessed by coaches and peers regularly is a strong motivation for this powerful team.

While Ladouceur acknowledges that the commitment card process can be tedious and time consuming, he is of the opinion that it is one significant component to the development of the young men in his program. Ladouceur believes that some coaches want to cut corners to avoid the monotony of the little things, like the commitment cards. However, this activity seems to contribute well to the program as a whole, and to the individuals involved. It is in part because of the time-consuming activities, such as commitment cards, that Ladouceur thinks having roughly fifty kids on a varsity program is close to the perfect number. If the number of players gets too large, it is too difficult, or impossible, to involve every individual with the time that is needed for overall development.

The Strength Program

MOST OPPOSING TEAMS look better and bigger than De La Salle teams in the tunnel prior to the game. The Spartans' offensive linemen average around two hundred-twenty pounds. It is important to note that the entire De La Salle football team, especially the linemen, is very strong. Most of the starting linemen, although undersized according to traditional standards, squat over five hundred pounds. Head Coach Bob Ladouceur says that he would put his team up against anyone else's from a physical strength standpoint. Usually, the De La Salle team has eight to ten guys per year who bench press over three hundred pounds.

When it comes to the weight room, Ladouceur believes many coaches use a lack of facilities as an excuse for why their programs aren't where they could be. Ladouceur believes a team doesn't need much in terms of facilities to run a proper strength and conditioning program. As a matter of fact, Ladouceur states that the biggest necessity is simply space.

De La Salle has generated a lot of training tools on its own, giving them what they need to train players, but at a lower cost than commercially made products. An example of this came from a time when Ladouceur and his coaches went to a junk yard and purchased some used tires. They were then able to make harnesses out of ropes for their players to use during speed training. Today, the program still uses this self-made training device to help the team improve in speed, power, and endurance.

When one walks into the weight room at De La Salle, there are no visible chairs or music in the background. Players understand that when they enter the weight room, it is time to train. It is remarkable that there is also very little talking amongst athletes in the weight room—they are very workman-like in attitude.

During the workouts, all of the exercises are on timers; this means that every second of rest between sets is monitored. During the football season, the team lifts two days a week— Tuesdays and Saturdays—and the players are remarkably able to increase their strength as the season carries on. The strength and conditioning program is not only something that benefits the program from a physical standpoint, but is also the single most important contributor to successful team-building, according to Coach Ladouceur.

The Leadership

HEAD COACH BOB Ladouceur believes that if a program is run the right way, with citizenship being a primary focus, wins and successes will follow. Ladouceur attempts to approach coaching from a purely educational perspective. With this outlook, De La Salle does not run athletes as a disciplinary action; rather, they sit them from playing in games. At De La Salle, team rules are applicable year-round, both on and off the campus. Ladouceur and his staff pursue all rumors aggressively. As a result, De La Salle regularly goes into their season opener with two or three players suspended from the first game for disciplinary reasons.

An example of the way De La Salle responds to a disciplinary situation is as follows: if a student is disrespectful in one of his classes during the off-season, he will be brought to meet with a member of the coaching staff and given one warning. If that player's behavior does not change, the ramification instituted will be that he will miss playing the season opener. As a result of this, the athletes entering the program understand that they must toe the line in order to be a member of De La Salle football.

The Team-Building

IN CONJUNCTION WITH commitment cards, De La Salle institutes many distinctive things in order to mold one hundred-eighty players into a united group where brotherhood is a more prevalent topic of discussion than is winning. Because the weight room program is organized in a manner that conveys to athletes that it is strictly a place of work, with well-organized and rigorous workouts, the athletes going through this training process become closely united to one another. Coach Ladouceur finds that through the demanding workouts and the level of commitment players make, they are heavily invested before the team takes its first snap of the season. Ladouceur believes that as a result of this process, his teams tend to compete harder and are less likely to accept defeat late in football games.

While Coach Ladouceur believes the single biggest team-builder is having a highly-organized and demanding off-season program, he thinks that fundraising for charity is an important team builder in itself. Ladouceur is convinced that coaches need to demonstrate to their players that they are about more than just football. If players perceive that football is everything to their coaches, they often will lose respect for them. Though this is not the primary motivation for Coach Ladouceur organizing fundraising activities for charities, it is a major outcome.

The De La Salle football program has one person who holds the title of the official team mom. This person coordinates with other parents to host team dinners every Thursday evening, the night before each football game. Each family only hosts one team dinner per season and foots the cost for the meal. It is in this informal setting at team dinners where the players assemble in groups and hold each other accountable regarding goals they had each set on their commitment cards the previous Friday.

The Boundaries

LIKE MANY TEAMS, De La Salle holds a parent meeting each season. At this meeting, Head Coach Bob Ladouceur sets forth some boundaries for parents that enable him and his staff to coach the players without undue interference. Ladouceur makes it clear to the parents that the best players will play in games. He then goes on to define the best players as the individuals who can perform what is asked of them with the greatest success rates. It is in part the reason that two hundred-twenty pound linemen are generally the type of players who start for the De La Salle Spartans. Then, offensive attacks that feature strong rushing attacks are built around these undersized linemen.

Ladouceur requests that parents permit players to experience the season on their own. He encourages parents to bond with other parents as they mutually enjoy their sons' football experiences. Ladouceur views high school football, and his program in particular, as a growing up period when the young men begin a vital maturation process that can be easily thwarted if parents interfere.

The Brotherhood

IN THE LOCKER room of the Spartans, a sign reads, "Brotherhood is Everything." At De La Salle, this is not just a fancy slogan but is a philosophy that impacts people and fosters relationships for years to come. An example of this is illustrated in a story told by current Jacksonville Jaguars running back, Maurice Jones-Drew, a former De La Salle Spartan. Jones-Drew relates a time when he was a De La Salle player, and one of his teammates rarely got playing time in games. He noted that like all of the players in the program, this teammate was going through the workouts day after day, alongside the starting players. Even though this player wasn't one of the high-end players from a talent standpoint, he was a critical component of a forged brotherhood—a brotherhood shaped through shared experiences at De La Salle. When Jones-Drew held his weekly radio show from Jacksonville, this former teammate would call every Tuesday night and converse with Jones-Drew for around thirty minutes each week. This player, like all of the Spartans, was received into the De La Salle brotherhood not because of his athletic talent, as is a prerequisite at many programs, but rather due to the uniqueness of the Spartan's focus on brotherhood and appreciation for various types of contributions that different teammates make.

Listening to Jones-Drew speak about his alma mater is an experience all of its own. The passion that Jones-Drew encompasses for his high school program is moving. It is evident that De La Salle and the coaching staff have strongly influenced his life and the lives of many others. The bond of this brotherhood is perhaps the largest contributor to the instantaneous friendships often formed across the country among former De La Salle players regardless of when they graduated. There is a connection at De La Salle that reaches beyond the gridiron and extends throughout the entire student body. As Jones-Drew put it, "Football is at such a surface level. We strive for greatness here at De La Salle, whether it is in the classroom, socially, [through] football, or becoming a man; we strive for greatness." If football is at the surface level, the brotherhood of De La Salle Spartans could be considered the foundation.

Head Coach Bob Ladouceur believes adolescents need as many positive and caring adults as possible in their lives to assist them in their maturation processes. Regardless of the environments and family circumstances in which children are raised, many people need to be involved in the growth and development of each individual. Ladouceur is grateful that his own children have coaches and other adults in their lives with whom they have established positive connections. Being part of the De La Salle family personifies the saying that *it takes a village to raise a child.*

The Assistants

WHEN BOB LADOUCEUR sets out to hire assistant coaches, he seeks coaches whom he doesn't have to instruct. With limited time, it is understandable that coaches who are gifted with the ability to create on their own are advantageous to any coaching staff. Ladouceur believes that coaching, like any other talent, is a gift. With his wealth of coaching experience, Ladouceur finds it very difficult to teach the game of football to someone who just doesn't get it. Ladouceur goes on to say that some people don't get chemistry, some people don't get math, and some people don't get football. Individuals who possess the capability to view the field well are a huge benefit to Ladouceur. Coach Landoucer acknowledges that it is rare to locate all of these characteristics in a single coach, but it certainly gives him the best kind of support when he comes across a coach who embodies all of them.

The Staff

BOB LADOUCEUR ATTRIBUTES much of his teams' successes to the consistency in both staff and philosophy. Many of the coaches on his staff are former players for De La Salle; when they begin coaching the Spartans, there is little or no learning curve as to how things are run in the program. One of the finest examples of this comes from Justin Alumbaugh. Alumbaugh first played offensive line at De La Salle during his high school years. As an alumnus, he coached alongside Ladouceur on the offensive line. A few years later, Ladouceur handed the offensive line job completely over to him. Additionally, Terry Eidson has been with Ladouceur for twenty-eight out of the twenty-nine years that Ladouceur has been at De La Salle. With coaches like Alumbaugh and Eidson, De La Salle has no problem getting the same time commitment, effort, and levels of exertion out of the players that they got fifteen years ago. While some things have changed in the program over the years, the work ethic of the players in the program and the expectations from the coaching staff have not. The maintenance of such harmony and reliability within the coaching staff is a huge contributor to the success of the De La Salle Spartans.

While Ladouceur will acknowledge that the type of offensive or defensive systems a program uses really doesn't matter that much, he believes that coaches must really know the systems they are running. Ladouceur claims that schemes coupled with the ability to outsmart an opponent are way overblown; however, coaches must know a system well. Ladouceur feels that if a coach doesn't know a system well, the players will quickly become aware of it. At De La Salle, players don't wear a wristband full of plays. Instead, they win using a system the coaches teach well, and the players execute well, including a strong emphasis on the fundamentals of the game.

High School Football in California

IN THE STATE of California, schools are allowed ten practices with only helmets for spring football. While some teams attend team football camps at universities, De La Salle hosts its own camp, just for linemen. In the fall, De La Salle is allowed two weeks of practice before a scrimmage against another school. Then, they are permitted one more week of practice prior to the first game. While most schools in California have athletic periods at the beginning or end of the school day, De La Salle is required to conduct all of their training before or after school. This training schedule is a result of the religion class that is required, as De La Salle is a private Catholic school. With this requirement, it becomes difficult to fit physical education classes into students' schedules.

According to the state of California, players must obtain a 2.0 GPA in order to maintain athletic eligibility. Because there are so many schools spanning the state of California, there are multiple state champions each year within the same classification. This amounts to teams competing for regional state championship each year; it wouldn't be feasible to host only one state championship in such a large state. Lastly, one distinctive aspect of Californian football is that junior varsity games are played on Friday evenings just before the varsity games.

Independence High School

Charlotte, North Carolina

Overview

WHEN TOM KNOTTS took over as the Head Football Coach at Independence High School in 2000 he located a second place trophy in the trophy case at the school. At Coach Knotts's first practice, he gathered his new team around the fence surrounding their practice field with the trophy in hand. With one swift motion, Knotts made a very dramatic first impression when he slung the trophy over the fence outlining the team's practice field. He followed this with the explanation that the team would not be content finishing second from that day forth. He shouted to his new team that they would only be satisfied with state championships, and no other second-place finishes would be applauded either internally or externally. From that point forth, Tom Knotts laid the foundation for one of the most remarkable runs in high school football history.

During his first season at Independence High School, Tom Knotts coached the future Florida Gator quarterback, Chris Leak, during his sophomore year. It was this first year with Coach Knotts that Independence claimed a state championship, having lost only the second game of the season. The subsequent season, Independence won another state championship, this time undefeated. For Leak's finale as a senior, the Independence Patriots claimed their third straight state title and went undefeated once again.

The following year, in 2003, Independence proved they could uphold this winning tradition without the much-heralded quarterback leading the team's offense. They once again went undefeated and claimed their fourth straight state championship. The Patriots then went forth to win the state championship in 2004, 2005, and 2006, making it seven in a row.

Traveling up north in the fall of 2007, the Patriots brought their 109 game winning streak with them to play Elder High School from Ohio. The game ended with Elder knocking off Independence 41-34. Independence then lost in the 2007 North Carolina State Title Game, thus ending their bid for an eighth consecutive state championship. Throughout their impeccable run, the Patriots finished in the top ten of the *USA Today* national poll for seven straight seasons, a feat no other team has accomplished this century. Teams that put together such phenomenal runs of success clearly have a solid foundation in place for getting there. Independence High School's Head Coach Tom Knotts attributes his team's success to four specific building blocks.

The Strength Program

TOM KNOTTS SAYS that even though Independence High School utilizes a specific way to train its athletes, the type of program a team follows is not what matters, what does matter is whether the program produces three key outcomes: strength, increased work ethic, and confidence development.

First, the most important facet of the strength program is that it must be designed with the purpose of preventing injuries. With the nature of the sport, injuries are going to occur, but the strength program must be something that minimizes the injuries sustained on a team. The next characteristic of a proper strength program is that it must increase the work ethic of the team. According to Coach Knotts, workouts need to be structured in such a way that the rigor put on the players develops solid work ethics. The last component of a quality strength program is that it must generate confidence within the individuals participating in the program. Coach Knotts states that though his team may not be the physically strongest team in North Carolina, his players believe that they are. It is interesting to note that two of the three ingredients of Coach Knott's successfully designed strength program are non-physical attributes (work ethic and confidence).

So, what does the strength program look like for the Independence Patriots? To start with, each of the fifty-five varsity players and seventy-five junior varsity players are required to take one weightlifting class each semester. These classes are instructed by members of the Patriots' coaching staff; Coach Knotts teaches two of them, the defensive coordinator teaches one, and the offensive line coach teaches one. Both in season and out of season, the team lifts weights five days each week. Within the five days per week, workouts are set on three-week cycles: lower-body workouts take place on Mondays and Thursdays, upper-body workouts take place on Tuesdays and Fridays, and workouts consisting of power clean variations as well as speed and agility training exercises take place on Wednesdays.

Mondays and Tuesdays are the traditional heavy-lifting days that most schools follow in standardized workouts; on Thursdays and Fridays, the workouts are unique to the program at Independence. During the Thursday and Friday workouts bar speed and explosiveness are emphasized. During these specialized training days, a typical workout has the athlete complete eight sets of three reps at fifty percent of his maximum, and then four sets of two reps at sixty percent of the athlete's maximum. Key to this training is ensuring that there are no more than forty-five seconds of rest in between the sets. At the end of each three-week cycle, players max out on the bench press *or* incline press, coupled with either squats *or* dead lifts. Results are updated at the conclusion of each three-week cycle and then displayed on the wall of the weight room.

Despite physical strength not being the primary focus of their workouts, the Patriots do achieve impressive numbers. The 2007 team included twenty-three players who could bench press three hundred pounds or more. It is even more remarkable that every varsity player power cleaned at least two hundred-five pounds during that season. Coach Knotts maintains that the decision to lift so aggressively during the season is primarily about creating a mindset. The type of opponent the team is playing on a Friday night will determine how rigorous the upper-body workout is on game day. If they are not playing a difficult opponent, the coaches will put the team through a very difficult workout. On the other hand, if they are playing a tough opponent, the coaches will back off a bit on game day, but still lift, because that is what they do.

The Summer Program

WHEN INDEPENDENCE HIGH School ends for the year in early June, they begin to pull away from their competition in the installation of their offense and defensive systems. At the beginning of summer, the Patriots begin practicing without pads four days a week while maintaining the weight room program. This four day a week practice schedule lasts until the fourth of July. From the fourth of July until the beginning of August, Independence then goes to practicing five times per week. At the beginning of August, practice officially begins for the state of North Carolina; by this time, Independence has a huge start on most of their competition. In the early years of Coach Knotts' tenure at Independence, the summer schedule provided a monumental advantage over their opponents. Now, many schools have implemented similar summer schedules in hopes of keeping up with the Patriots.

The Schemes

WITH SO MUCH time being dedicated during the summer, the Patriots become very efficient at their single back offense and 4-3 defense. Most teams find it difficult to compete with the depth of their offensive and defensive systems alone. The Patriots' offense is one that utilizes multiple personnel groupings to create mismatches against its opponents. The Patriots use one and two tight end sets with multiple motion packages. As a direct result of the Patriot's offensive success, this system is one that is becoming more and more familiar across the state of North Carolina. Like most teams, Independence places great trust in the systems they run, and believe that schemes play a large role in the success they have enjoyed during the last eight seasons.

The Coaches

THE COACHING STAFF at Independence High school consists of seven paid coaches and two or three volunteers each year. This is a small staff when compared with many other top high schools. Even with a limited staff, the varsity coaches develop the junior varsity players as well; this means that the seventy-five junior varsity players practice alongside the varsity players. Obviously, the junior varsity players are not going to get as much focus as the varsity players get on Mondays, Tuesdays, or Wednesdays of a game week. As a result, the varsity staff is very involved in the coaching of the junior varsity games on Thursday evenings.

Coach Knotts says that the coaches do a whole lot more teaching on Thursday nights than on Friday nights. The reason for this is that the varsity team is so well prepared, that very little correcting needs to be done during a typical Friday night game. The coaches do, however, pour themselves into the development of the junior varsity players during their games on Thursdays. This gives the junior varsity players a big advantage when they become varsity players down the road.

Corrective Mondays

WITH A PROGRAM that rarely loses, it can be difficult to scrutinize the Friday night victory as closely as a coaching staff does following a Friday night loss. On Mondays following Friday night's game, the Independence coaching staff are ready to dissect the game film after a weekend of reviewing it. While a portion of the coaching staff is on the field with the junior varsity players, a portion of the varsity players are in with Coach Knotts and their position coach reviewing each group's performance. It is worth noting that each review session takes as long as needed in order to correct the shortcomings of the game. After one position is done, the next group of players comes in to watch their performances with their position coach and the head coach. This routine is repeated three more times until the entire varsity team has watched their game with their position coach and the head coach.

Throughout the examining of the film, a detailed list is kept for major mistakes during the game; such mistakes include: fumbles, penalties, loafing, and major assignment errors. For each of these mistakes, the team runs a two hundred yard sprint at the conclusion of Monday's practice. All players know that Monday two hundreds are a familiar consequence for Independence football. The total number of two hundreds the team will run on any given Monday never exceeds eight; this was not always the case. In earlier years, Coach Knotts would have a much higher cap, as the team would sometimes run as much as fifteen two hundreds on Mondays.

The idea of two hundreds might seem insignificant to an outside observer, but the Independence coaching staff drew a direct correlation between running the two hundreds and the statistic that the 2005 team played an entire season without fumbling once.

The Staff

IN THE TWENTY-SIX years Tom Knotts has been a head coach, he has only conducted around five formal interviews for assistant coaches. When he needs to hire an assistant coach, he prefers to hire someone with whom he already has established a relationship—somebody he knows well. At Independence, Coach Knotts has formed an agreement with the current principal that allows him to have five assistant coaches in the building as teachers. This arrangement will last until the day he brings somebody in who does not teach in the classroom well. With that in mind, he cautiously chooses his coaches as to not cost him this privilege in the future.

Knotts has a philosophy that each high school program needs four top-notch coaches. If the head coach is the offensive coordinator, the staff must also provide an offensive line coach, a defensive coordinator, and a defensive position coach that are all high quality coaches. The defensive position coach needs to be very adept at that position so that the defensive coordinator can rely on two of the three defensive position groups being coached at a very high level. The offensive line coach is also an extremely valuable position for Knotts, and could easily be viewed as equivalent to either of the coordinator spots.

After the four "top-notch" spots are staffed, Coach Knotts maintains that each coach can benefit from younger coaches who are hard workers and teachable. Young coaches tend to be moldable and do not bring in solidified philosophies that might clash with an established system. Additionally, with evolving technology in the game of high school football, having coaches on staff who are skilled with current technology offers an additional benefit. According to Knotts, it is imperative to not have too many chiefs on a staff if a program is already navigating in a successful direction. Too many conflicts in methodology could cause unneeded tension and generate unnecessary distractions. The final thing Coach Knotts views as a major bonus is when the head track coaching position is reserved for an assistant football coach. The two sports work so closely together that both can benefit from an arrangement where a football coach doubles as the head track coach.

The Facilities

THE FOOTBALL PROGRAM'S booster club at Independence High School is linked to a booster club which funds all sports at the school. It is clear that financial resources have not played much of a role in the achievements of the football program. Around three dozen hard-working parents help to relieve some of the burden of the head coach by taking care of a wide variety of tasks, but not as much in a fiscal manner. It would be fair to rate the facilities at the school as mediocre at best. Though the weight room is larger than average, most of the equipment is old and run down. Also, the stadium lacks the capacity to host some of the popular home games for Independence. The games that look to draw bigger crowds are played at the County Stadium. Even with the lack of resources that some other top schools enjoy, Independence home games still have the ability to draw anywhere between twenty-five hundred and fifteen thousand fans.

The Top

COACH KNOTTS FIRMLY believes that it is harder to stay at the top than to make the initial journey there. This difficulty comes from the internal factors working against a program, not because a top team is every opponent's biggest game. Knotts stresses that when a credible coach takes over a new program, he has a certain shock factor working to his advantage. In other words, players instantly buy into the new philosophy and demands of a new coach. After awhile, however, a coach loses that shock factor, resulting in complacency that has a tendency to infiltrate a successful program. This becomes something that then must be confronted on a daily basis by the coaching staff. Coach Knotts even states that when a coach has been at a program for six or seven years, it is a good idea for that coach to begin again at a new school to eliminate some of the above factors.

Recruiting

WITH THE SUCCESS that Independence has seen spanning the past eight seasons, one would assume that they are sending off huge numbers of Division One players each year. On the contrary, the largest number of Division One scholarships in one recruiting class over the past eight years at Independence has been three. It is worth noting, however, that the last four recruiting classes have sent fifty-seven players to receive scholarships at the Division Two level or higher.

Jenks High School

Jenks, Oklahoma

Overview

WHEN JENKS HIGH School was seeking a new football coach after their 1995 season, they almost missed the very opportunity that resulted in turning their football program into a national powerhouse. Allan Trimble, Jenks' offensive coordinator for the previous three seasons, had recently accepted a job in Kansas, working in the business sector. After four months at his new job, the then 32-year-old Trimble was persuaded to return to Jenks—as the head coach. Over the next twelve seasons, the Jenks Trojans captured nine 6A state championships.

The decision to hire Coach Trimble not only positioned Jenks as the Oklahoma program that everybody was chasing, but it also catapulted Jenks to national stardom with both third and second place national rankings respectively in 2000 and 2001; this was according to *USA Today*. Throughout the past twelve years, Jenks has signed three to four Division One players per year. Players, however, have not been the only ones benefiting from the program's success—nine of Jenks' assistant coaches have become head coaches at other schools during the past twelve seasons.

College-like facilities, coupled with an annual football budget of more than one hundred thousand dollars, gives the impression of a college program on a slighter scale. The rather large single-high-school-district still emanates the feeling of a small town on Friday nights—the only place to be is the local football game. Another aspect to the small-town feel is the rivalry that exists between Jenks School District, and bordering Union School District. This rivalry could arguably be labeled the greatest high school football rivalry in present-day America. Even with the stellar facilities, generous budget, strong community support, and traditional rivalry, the core success to Jenks football success lies in their emphasis on team building.

Team Building

COACH TRIMBLE STANDS behind the statement that team building is the most important aspect of any successful team. He also adds that if this isn't made the number one priority for the team, the team cannot be successful. Trimble's belief in team building is supported by numerous illustrations throughout his coaching history when teams with high levels of talent did not function in a unified manner and were unable to grasp success. He also notes that teams with seemingly less talent in comparison to their opponents were able to excel after bonds were formed amongst players. Though Coach Trimble acknowledges that there are many different ways a coach can accomplish this objective, the importance of team building should not be downplayed.

Coach Trimble uses a variety of methods to shape his team into a unified group, thus enabling them to demonstrate cohesiveness on and off the field. Initially, the players participate in summer workouts just like teams all across the county. However, Jenks also begins their summer-pride workouts at 6:00 AM. The theory behind this is that it forces players to endure difficulty together, strengthening commitment to the team. Next, the juniors and seniors participate in either a paintball event or a ropes course alongside the coaches. This is designed to forge cooperation. Lastly, the seniors attend a retreat each summer. At the retreat, held in late July, the athletes participate in: water skiing, fishing, video game tournaments, and other traditional camp activities. A highlight of this experience is annual goal setting around a campfire.

To become a Trojan captain, one must go through a thorough and rigorous process including: applying for the position with a résumé, writing a letter of interest, generating a statement of goals, and proposing a plan of action. Additionally, the applicants will participate in an interview process beginning in early June. At this time, the eligible candidates will be given a list of responsibilities that will provide platforms from which they can demonstrate leadership to both their teammates as well as their coaches.

Two important responsibilities generally include setting examples of leadership in the weight room and contributing to a community service project. It is worth noting that the players are responsible to take the initiative to select their own service project.

Late in the summer, candidates are put through final formal interviews with the coaching staff. At these interviews, the candidates are asked direct questions that are often revealing. Five example questions from this interview process are:

1. *Would you rather choose to be an All-District and All-State player or part of a District and State Championship team?*
2. *If a teammate was contributing a poor effort in a drill with you present, how would you address it?*
3. *Who are some former captains that you think performed exceptional jobs? What made them successful?*
4. *What plans do you have to show our newcomers that they are now in our family? How do you convey what is expected of them?*

5. *If you were attempting to correct a teammate and he refused to respond to you, what would you do?*

After the final interviews, the coaching staff then ranks the candidates according to how well they are speculated to perform as captains. The selected captains are then put through extensive leadership training and entrusted with a great measure of responsibility for the Trojan football program.

The Program

HEAD COACH ALLAN Trimble controls the eighth grade through senior football programs at Jenks High School. These five grade levels contribute a combined total of two hundred-fifty to two hundred-sixty football players per year. The varsity team consists of around one hundred players; they all practice together. From these one hundred players some will participate in the ten game junior varsity schedule; between four and six additional sophomore games are also scheduled each year to allow more playing time for some of the junior varsity players.

The high school staff is compiled of nine district-paid assistants who are currently employed at Jenks High School; they are paid in the range of forty-five hundred to five thousand dollars per year. Additionally, the high school staff has five coaches under the classification of "jumped contracts." Jumped contracts are contracts funded by the booster club—it is a requirement that jumped contracts are equivocal to district-paid contracts. Capping off the contracts at Jenks High school, the Head Coach at Jenks earns fifteen thousand dollars in addition to his salary as Director of Football Operations.

With the fourteen assistants and the Head Coach, the Jenks program totals fifteen coaches for the span of grades ten through twelve. It is required that all of the coaches and players participate in a one hour athletic period year-round. The only exception to this is during the off-season when some coaches coach other sports. Regardless of additional coaching jobs for some of the assistants, the offensive, defensive, and special teams coordinators coach *only* football; this enables them to work with the football players year-round during sixth period at Jenks.

Jenks also runs a freshman academy on campus, adjacent to the high school. The freshman players practice separately from the high school team—they have their own field. The roughly seventy freshmen attend practices together, but are separated into varsity or junior varsity freshman teams for the season; each team plays eight games. Coaching the freshman are six coaches who each earn twenty-five hundred dollars per season.

The eighth grade program consists of eighty to ninety players. These players are split into three teams, one of which is the eighth grade junior varsity team. Each of the three eighth grade teams play eight games during the season and each have two coaches. With such a substantial number of games for the entire program, joined with twenty-seven coaches, Jenks demonstrates a very strong retention of players within their program.

Nearly six hundred youth participate in the first through seventh grade Mighty Might's program. Coach Trimble and his staff provide support to this program in a variety of ways. First, the youth coaches are given presentation materials and a smaller-sized playbook for the youth program, as well as drills and other helpful items for coaching a youth football team. Next, the high school staff hosts two Monday Night Madness sessions. At these three-hour sessions, the youth coaches come to the high school facility to participate in an offensive clinic on one night, and a defensive clinic on the other night. Lastly, the high school staff maintains an open-door policy with the youth coaches. This open-door policy allows the youth coaches to attend high school practices, film sessions, or workouts. It also permits them to just stop by the coaches' offices anytime to ask questions or solicit advice.

The Correlation Success

JENKS HAS NOT only been dominant on the gridiron, but has also been an elite program in track and field. The Trojans have won eight out of the last eleven state track championships—this success has a direct correlation with the success of the football program. The current head track coach was previously the football team's running back coach. Despite not coaching football at this time, he contributes to the football program by leading the football team through speed and conditioning training during the summer workouts.

It is estimated that between twenty and thirty percent of the Trojan football players participate on the track team. Generally speaking, half of the skill players take part in track, and some other players compete in throwing events also. If a football player is in need of additional speed development in order to increase his chances of getting on the football field, he is strongly encouraged to participate in track. Additionally, football players who are good enough to score points for the track team will be encouraged to participate in track. The harmony between the football and track programs at Jenks is one key to the impressive runs that the school has enjoyed in both sports.

The Community

JENKS, OKLAHOMA EMANATES a feeling of a warm, small-town community, which has miraculously been retained, in spite of the high school population growing to 2,950 students. Head Coach Allan Trimble boasts of the outstanding support of the school board and school administration. In this town, parents expect and support the coaches to train their kids hard. As a result, the football players participate in very demanding workouts. During the summer months, workouts begin at 6:00 AM, four days per week. This could be one reason why the Trojans have fewer varsity players in their program than do most of the surrounding schools. It is clear that in order to be a Jenks' football player, one must exemplify a strong work ethic and an unwavering dedication.

When football players exit the program, they often maintain strong ties to the school and program. Two examples of this can be observed in Jenks' alumni, Rocky Calmus and Shawn Mahan. Calmus, who after finishing a great career at Jenks, went on to win a national championship at the University of Oklahoma and was a Butkis Award winner before heading to the NFL. Mahan departed Jenks to become a three-year-starter at Notre Dame; he is currently a starting offensive lineman for the Pittsburgh Steelers. Both Calmus and Mahan have given back to Jenks with their time and finances; this seems to indicate that Jenks is as much of a part of them as they are to Jenks.

The Plan

ACCORDING TO STATE Regulations, a student athlete in Oklahoma must be passing all of his current classes in order to maintain athletic eligibility. As a result of this strict policy, grades are checked on a weekly basis with the intention that athletes won't be able to slip too far in the classroom without the problem being addressed. In order to assist students in achieving high standards in the classroom, thus ensuring that athletic eligibility is not lost, the Jenks' coaching staff has established a system to monitor this matter. One of the assistant coaches doubles as faculty liaison, which in itself amounts to a full-time job from a time commitment standpoint. This coach obtains a printout of the grades for each of the team's players every Wednesday. This faculty liaison is also responsible for communicating with teachers on a weekly basis to see which players may need extra help in their classes. Students who need extra help in their classes are then paired with the appropriate tutors, though most of the tutors will be paid for by the individual families. Some athletes who are in need of tutors are also given the opportunity to work with Key Club members at Jenks. The Jenks' Key Club is assembled of Advanced Placement students who tutor other students and receive credit for community service in exchange. Another strategy to keep grades high is the mandatory participation in study halls twice per week. Jenks' system to maintain athletic eligibility is superior to most of their competition.

Two-A-Days

INSTEAD OF THE traditional two-a-day practices that most teams hold, Jenks take an unorthodox approach, which Head Coach Allan Trimble believes aids his players and coaches in starting fresher in the season. Trimble's session begins at 7:30 AM and concludes at noon. From 7:30-9:10 AM, the team practices for one hour and forty minutes before a twenty minute break; this is when team mothers provide snacks for the team. From 9:30-10:00 AM, the players break up into their offensive or defensive position groups for either film or scheme installations. It is important to note that they rarely meet longer than thirty minutes for film sessions because they feel they begin to lose the attention of the players if the sessions last longer than thirty minutes. From that thirty minute position meeting or film session, the players return to the field for a second practice from 10:00-11:10 AM. From 11:10-11:30 AM the players break and consume oranges and bananas that are provided for the team. During the final thirty minutes, the team has a special team's practice where they cover two phases of the kicking game. The total session concludes at noon.

The Change

THE VAST MAJORITY of Jenks' opponents during their impressive twelve-year-run have had separate offenses and defenses. For the first ten years of the Jenks run with Head Coach Allan Trimble, the Trojans had their players playing both offense and defense. After losing a few games late during the 2004 and 2005 seasons, the program reexamined itself. The coaches concluded that their players were too tired and beaten down by the end of the season; this resulted in them not playing to their fullest potential when it counted the most. Consequently, the program now has nearly all players, except three or four, playing only one side of the football. The three or four who crossover still retain primary positions, but will sometimes be used in special situations on the other side of the ball. The side of the ball that an athlete best fits is generally determined by their coaches during the player's sophomore year. This reevaluation process that the Trojan coaches underwent illustrates that even the best programs can benefit from being open-minded to change, and being willing to adapt traditional aspects of their program when needed.

The Rivalry

NO OTHER STATE in the country has witnessed such dominance from two teams, at the highest classification, as Oklahoma has in Jenks and Union High Schools. These bordering school district programs are separated by a short four miles. In the last twelve seasons, Jenks and Union are the only schools to have held the 6A state championship trophy at the seasons' end. The games between the two rivals have exploded since the first sellout in 1994. Since their rival game quickly outgrew both of their home stadiums, it was relocated to the University of Tulsa's Chapman Stadium. This game, nicknamed the Backyard Bowl, was attended by 40,035 fans in 1999. In 2006, Sports Illustrated wrote that it was arguably the number one high school football rivalry in the nation.

Jenks nets around one hundred seventy-five thousand dollars per season if they are the visitor for the Union High School game. The years that they are the home team in the Union game, they bring in between two hundred fifty-five thousand dollars and two hundred seventy-five thousand dollars. Though these are extremely high numbers for high school football, the draw of this game can be seen when it is noted that seventeen of the last twenty-four meetings between the schools have been decided by ten points or fewer. These two programs clearly feed off of each other. An example of this came when Union added a 20 million dollar Multipurpose Activity Center to their campus; Jenks countered this with their own outstanding facility. The voters in Union passed two consecutive bonds which funded the facility; voters in Jenks countered this by passing a bond that funded Jenks' facility. It is apparent that the Jenks/Union rivalry is the best high school football rivalry of its class.

The Facility

THE ROBERT L. Sharp Health and Fitness Center is located in one of the end zones of the Jenks football stadium. The thirty-six thousand square foot facility cost around 5 million dollars. Bonds paid for the construction cost of the structure, with the Jenks football booster club and NFL alumni contributing half of the four hundred thousand dollar cost of the weight room equipment.

Inside of the three-story building lies: a weight room, separate varsity and junior varsity locker rooms, and equipment room. The second story of the center is home to a fitness center, and beautiful training room, among other amenities. The training room contains a state-of-the-art hydrotherapy pool with an underwater treadmill that goes up to seven miles per hour. The price tag of the hydrotherapy pool alone was fifty thousand dollars. This was one of the things, in addition to the outstanding training room staff, that Head Coach Allan Trimble credits for allowing Jenks to finish the 2007 season with *all* of the starting players still healthy.

The top story of the building is comprised of coaches' offices, team meeting rooms, and a banquet hall for team meetings and meals. Flat screen televisions are also mounted on some of the walls throughout the facility. This is not just a place that players consider as home, but it has actually turned into a place where kids spend time together on Saturdays watching football games or get an occasional Madden tournament going with the multiple televisions and projectors. This is truly a breathtaking structure and design which is nearly unfathomable in a high school setting.

Oklahoma High School Football

IN THE STATE of Oklahoma, each school is permitted to spend up to one hour a day during school hours working on football-related activities; the condition is that they can't have any pads involved. This, of course, is in addition to the ten two-hour padded practices permitted for spring football. After school is released for the summer, schools are also allowed to participate in a team camp. Jenks used to go to the University of Tulsa team camp, but they have recently made the switch to hosting camp at their own school. The switch allows for the ten schools that participate in the camp, Jenks included, to pay much cheaper rates while gaining more individualized coaching than at the university camp.

Football in the fall always begins on the second Tuesday in August. During each preseason, Jenks have an intersquad scrimmage on the Saturday after their first fall practice. The following Friday, they play a scrimmage against another school, followed by a three-team scrimmage the subsequent Friday where each team plays one half. In the three preseason scrimmages before the season opener, the Jenks Trojans rest their franchise players in order to avoid the risk of injury. In all, the Trojans will have sixteen fall practices and three scrimmages before they hit the field for their season opener.

Carroll High School

Southlake, Texas

Overview

CARROLL HIGH SCHOOL, located in Southlake, Texas, was the second team in Texas High School history to win three straight large classification (5A) titles. The Dragons also won four state titles in five years in an unprecedented run from 2002–2006. On top of that, the Carroll Dragons have earned two national championships in 2004 and 2006, and a second place finish in 2005; this is all according to USA Today.

In Southlake, Texas, the Carroll Dragons are the hottest ticket in town. As a matter of fact, the day before season tickets go on sale, fans line up around the block hoping to be one of the twelve thousand fans granted the opportunity to watch the Dragons defeat their opponents at Dragon Stadium. Perhaps the reason for such a huge fan following comes from the fact that the Dragons have not lost one home game in the past six seasons.

The Carroll players are accustomed to playing games in front of crowds much larger than the regular twelve thousand fans at each of their home games. In 2006, Carroll played Miami Northwestern in front of over thirty thousand paid fans at Southern Methodist University's stadium; they also played in front of just under fifty thousand fans in 2006 against then undefeated Euless Trinity—this game was held at Texas Stadium.

At the beginning of the program's successful run, the predominantly Caucasian team found themselves having difficulty convincing college recruiters that they could play at the next level. Recruiters seemed to label the Dragon players as overachievers and kids who were products of the system—they believed they would be risky investments for college programs. Today, colleges are aggressively recruiting Carroll football athletes.

In 2005, Carroll produced a double digit number of Division One scholarships. Head Coach Hal Wasson is adamant that the characterization of Dragon players as overachievers is inaccurate; he believes this of players of other schools as well. Wasson supposes that players either reach their potentials or they don't. He is very direct in stating that he believes there are many underachievers in football and life, but he doesn't believe that the notion of an overachiever exists. It is in part that mindset—a different lens through which to view the overachiever debate—that has contributed to the success of the Carroll Dragons' football program.

The Program

ACCORDING TO COACH Hal Wasson, the most important prerequisites to being a member of the Carroll football program are being both one hundred percent unselfish and team-oriented. One of the ways the players are molded into these two forms is through what is called the Dragon Maker phase of the Carroll offseason program; this training program closely resembles a boot camp for the team. The Dragon Maker program begins around one week after basketball season ends and takes place during the players' athletic period of the school day.

During the Dragon Maker program, there are three components to each of the workouts. The first component is a fifteen to twenty minute weight room workout where high reps structure each set with short rest periods between sets. The second component is a fifteen to twenty minute station where players are put through a simplistic but demanding pushup and sit-up station. The last component consists of seven different stations including mat drills and change of directions drills; this is held in the indoor football facility. Each of these seven stations is conducted for approximately ninety seconds. Throughout each of the three components of the Dragon Maker program, everything is executed simultaneously, and on command. For example, the players must get down at the same time for the pushups and sit-ups and stand up at the same time—this is similar to boot camp. If the players don't perform correctly and together, the process starts over.

A foundational part of the Dragon Maker program comes with the understanding that each athlete is both a worker and an encourager throughout the entire workout. This facet of the Dragon Maker program is where the athletes are molded into unselfish players. Clearly, all the players work very hard throughout the drills. However, when a player is on the short break between drills, though extremely tired and just trying to survive, he must find it within himself to verbally encourage others who are currently going through the drills.

The daily discipline of this program is designed to continue for as long as it takes for every team member to get on the same page. When all of the drills are performed with exact precision, the Dragon Maker phase will end. This usually takes around seven days with a strong team; it can take up to three weeks for teams that struggle more.

Team members know at the end of each workout whether or not they have met the Dragon Maker expectations. Often, the coaches will simply tell the team that the majority of the team is doing fine but they still have some players who haven't figured it out yet. The coaches are in agreement that it isn't profitable for the team to name names; rather, they leave it up to the players to get each other in line. Through the Dragon Maker program, players are forced to either get on board with the direction and purpose of the program, or get out of the way.

The Attack Teams

ONE OF THE key components to Carroll football victory comes from the scout teams—Carroll calls them attack teams. Head Coach Hal Wasson is quick to point out that the attack teams have played a huge role in the team's success; he says that the Carroll attack teams really work their tails off. Players entering the program understand that participating on the attack teams is part of the price they have to pay in order to be a Dragon. It would be fair to say that nearly all of the big time players who have come through the program have contributed at one time on the attack teams. The intensity of competition at practice is exceedingly high because the effort of the attack teams is at such a high level. Varsity players cannot disengage for even one play during practice, or they will get beat by the opposing member of the attack team.

Service to the team is not the only reward for great effort on the attack teams. Each week, the three attack team players of the week from offense, defense, and special teams will serve as three of the captains for the varsity game on Friday night. The same player might very well be a captain three weeks in a row if he is the attack team player of the week three weeks in a row. The coaching staff *doesn't* try to rotate who the attack team players of the week are from week to week; whoever earns the honor each week is granted the captain privilege.

Another incentive for attack team members is that the members of each attack team earn the same number of reward stickers for their helmets as the offense, defense, or special teams units whom they prepared for the varsity game. For example, if the offensive unit earns stickers for Friday night's game, the defensive attack unit who helped prepare them will earn an equal number of stickers.

Lastly, with each play at practice being filmed and evaluated by the coaching staff, an attack team player will occasionally move his way up the depth chart based on the filmed practices. This elevates the competition level at practice since the attack players will sometimes be rewarded with varsity playing time based on practice performances. This consistent competition amongst players, coupled with the unity in teamwork, serves as a major contributor to the Dragons' success on the gridiron.

The Off-season Program

DURING THE OFF-SEASON, athletes have to split into groups out of sheer necessity. With over four hundred players spanning the ninth through twelfth grade program, it is easy to see why dividing the players into groups is essential for success. One group will lift weights on Monday, Wednesday, and Friday during the first rotation week. Then, that group will lift weights on Tuesday and Thursday the following week. Meanwhile, the other group will train opposite of the first group. On days when players are not in the weight room, they participate in speed and agility training, or mat drills. A large component of the Carroll speed program is the running of two hundreds. Players are divided into position groups for the two hundreds and each player has to make his target time in the two hundreds or his entire group has to run again. As a result of the two hundreds, the Dragons are an exceedingly well-conditioned team; even the offensive and defensive linemen don't carry much unnecessary weight on their bodies.

The Team-Building

THERE ARE THREE ways the members of the Carroll Dragon football program are united through team building. The first way is through a character curriculum that takes about twenty to thirty minutes per day—each of the four hundred plus players takes part. The second area is through the summer strength and conditioning program. Unlike most programs, Carroll does not make the summer program mandatory, but kids elect to train together and hold each other accountable for their attendance during the summer program. The last way the Dragons are brought close together is through their original approach to an annual team meeting.

This team meeting is held each year after the inter-squad scrimmage in the fall. Following the scrimmage, Head Coach Hal Wasson, along with the members of the varsity team, close themselves in the locker room for what often turns out to be a six hour closed-door dialogue. The meeting begins with Coach Wasson sharing information about himself. These topics often include: his goals, his expectations, something about his family, and unique facts about his life. After Wasson is finished talking, players are given the opportunity to share.

The football athletes at Carroll are all expected to share something personal about themselves, as well as how long they have been at Carroll. Players are also encouraged to lay everything on the table. If there are strained relationships between players, or if players harbor criticism of a teammates' work ethic, this is the venue that Coach Wasson has chosen to deal with it in a direct manner. Two unique characteristics of most of the Dragon players are that they tend to have thick skins and exemplify adult-like maturity while still in high school. Coach Wasson views these team meetings as advantageous going into the season because they find solutions, therefore minimizing potential distractions before the upcoming season.

The Quarterbacks

MUCH OF THE success of Carroll football can be attributed to the quarterbacks who have guided one of the most prolific offenses in high school football history. The past four quarterbacks to direct the Carroll offense include: Chase Wasson (Texas State University), Chase Daniel (University of Missouri), Greg McElroy (University of Alabama), and Riley Dodge (University of North Texas). All four quarterbacks share two crucial characteristics. First, all four exemplify mental toughness. Second, they all are very athletic quarterbacks.

While examining this talent closely, one will see that three of these quarterbacks were starting wide receivers for the Dragons prior to becoming the starting quarterback. In fact, Chase Daniel played as a receiver for Chase Wasson; Riley Dodge played as a wide receiver for Greg McElroy prior to becoming the signal caller of the Dragon offense. The athleticism is imperative in the no huddle spread offense that Carroll runs because they rely on their quarterbacks to be dual threats. Each year when the Dragons begin their practices, they aspire for at least two thousand yards passing, and at least one thousand yards rushing from their quarterback.

In the Spring of 2002, former Head Coach Todd Dodge, current Head Coach Hal Wasson, former wide receiver coach Clayton George, and the offensive line coach for Carroll all traveled to Middle Tennessee State University (MTSU) to learn more about the no huddle spread offense that MTSU was running. On the drive home, the four coaches actually generated their own hand signals. The implementation of this system has been fundamental to achieving the tremendous success the program has enjoyed since the spread offense was implemented in 2002. It has assisted the Dragons in winning four out of five state championships from 2002-2006.

In 2007, the Dragons averaged five hundred-seventeen yards of offense; over two hundred yards were on the ground, and over three hundred yards were through the air. This system has not only assisted the team in moving the ball efficiently, but it has also allowed Carroll to dictate the pace of the game. Similarly to the way basketball teams try to control the tempo of the game, Carroll also utilizes these principles in the game of football. Additionally, the system allows them to minimize the number of substitutions that defenses can make throughout a game. With such an increased success since the implementation of this offense in 2002, players as early as second grade can be seen in the shotgun spread preparing for years down the road when they will run the same system.

The Coaches

WHEN IT COMES to hiring coaches, Head Coach Hal Wasson is effectively organized, has a clear idea of what he wants, and has completed his background homework. Character traits are the number one ingredient he is seeking. Coach Wasson's expectations for each candidate include: loyalty, trustworthiness, a strong work ethic, and a passion for coaching. Another key ingredient that Coach Wasson looks for in an assistant coach is an individual who doesn't wear his feelings on his sleeve. Coach Wasson describes an ideal potential coach as a hungry individual who really desires to be in his respective coaching position. Wasson also stands behind the philosophy that a great teacher makes a great coach.

Coach Wasson's style is such that he does not use a set script of questions and states that he will not interview over the phone. He believes that the level of self confidence of a potential coach can be best assessed during a face-to-face interview. If a coach has previously worked for a coach who carries a well-respected reputation, that speaks loudly to Wasson.

One thing that sets Wasson apart in his hiring of an assistant coach is that he will go to great lengths to contact someone *not* on the candidate's reference sheet if he feels he will get more candid answers. From this conversation, he really strives to determine how the individual responds when things *aren't* going well. Wasson seeks coaches who display absolute loyalty and trustworthiness in times of adversity. While Wasson admits it is important to not have all of the coaches similar in personalities and coaching styles, he must have loyalty and trustworthiness from his coaches—after all, he expects the same of his players.

The Robinhood District

IN THE STATE of Texas, wealthy school districts are mandated to send money to the state in order that it will be fairly distributed to poorer districts. Carroll Independent School District comprises an extremely high tax base. It doesn't take a long drive in Southlake, Texas to recognize that this is an extremely affluent area. As one of the wealthiest areas in Texas, Southlake falls on the giving side of the Robinhood Program. Carroll Independent School District actually sent 17 million dollars to the state to be distributed to other school districts. On the other side of the Robinhood Program, the receivers of these funds will often have nice stadiums that go unfilled on Friday nights. Yet, as part of the distribution from the Robinhood Program, wealthy districts are mandated to send funds to the state in order to help out poorer school districts in the area of funding.

Katy High School

Katy, Texas

Overview

THE KATY TIGERS have been a dominant program for many years. From 2003–2007 the team established a record of 70-5; this includes two 5A state championships in 2003 and 2007. Since the debut of its football program, Katy High School has won three earlier state championships with titles in 1959, 1997, 2000. In nine out of the last ten years, the team has reached at least the state quarterfinal round of the playoffs.

The roughly three hundred-fifty ninth through twelfth graders playing Katy football come from a predominantly blue-collar community. Within the Katy Independent School district, there are other high schools with more affluent backgrounds than Katy. It seems that the blue-collar mentality is a significant key to understanding the foundation of the Katy football program. The ten thousand seat Rhodes Stadium is sold out for all games, and ticket prices have not increased since the mid-1980s. In 2007, if tickets were available for purchase, one could watch the game for only four dollars.

The Program

HEAD COACH GARY Joseph attributes his program's success to two key areas. The first area is faith. On one hand, the majority of the kids in the Katy program have a strong faith in God—this was instilled in them from their parents at young ages. This mutual faith creates a natural unity among the players. Additionally, the parents place strong faith in the coaches and entrust the coaches to perform their jobs with very little negative interference. The second key to the success of the Katy program is the established tradition. The strong tradition of the program results in players not wanting to be part of a group that brings any dishonor to the program; the athletes don't take what they have for granted.

The Katy High School team has only one middle school that fully feeds into Katy High School; two other middle schools contribute a portion of their students. This is not an ideal scenario for Coach Joseph who has no control over the middle school programs. Most other 5A schools in Texas have much control over their feeding programs in terms of offensive and defensive systems run as well as the hiring of coaches. Katy, however, compensates other ways.

Attracting assistant coaches with high salaries is not part of Katy football. The assistant coaches earn no more than fifty-five hundred dollars each for coaching at Katy. Throughout Texas, most schools pay much higher coaching stipends. The coaches who make up the staff at Katy hold great appreciation for both the program and the community at large. On average, Katy produces one Division One player per year—this is far fewer than many expect from such a dominant program.

The Athletes

TO BE PART of the Katy football program in the fall, an athlete must participate during the entire off-season program. This is a rule that Coach Joseph has instituted; he will only compromise this policy for athletes who move into the area late, thus hindering their abilities to participate throughout the off-season program. About eighty percent of the Katy track team is composed of football players. One of the assistant football coaches doubles as the head track coach; three other assistant football coaches double as track coaches as well. With this relationship between the football and track programs, both programs profit from each other.

Part of the preparation of athletes during the off-season comes from their work in the weight room. On average, about eight players each year bench press over three hundred pounds; around six will be able to full squat at least four hundred pounds. According to Katy football, full squats are defined as the athlete's middle of the thigh being parallel with the ground.

One of the player-initiated team-building traditions at Katy High School is the unity circle. During pregame, at both home and away games, the Tiger athletes huddle just inside their side of the fifty-yard line without the coaches present; it is here that they form a unity circle. Inside of the circle, the players hold an open forum where they share what they are thinking. This usually includes such things as the importance or expectations of the game at hand.

The Population Changes

WHEN MIKE JOHNSTON took over the Katy football program in 1980, Katy felt the effects of fewer students due to a new high school that had opened in the district. The decrease in population, however, wasn't enough to move Katy down in classification—they had to continue playing at the same level, but with fewer athletes.

From 1982–1984 Katy won no more than three games in each of those seasons. In 1985, they improved with four wins. In 1986, the program went through their regular season with an undefeated 10-0 record before losing in the playoffs. Twenty-two years later, the Tigers have not had a losing season since 1985. In recent history, they have taken their dominance to a new level by advancing to the state quarterfinals in nine out of the last ten years. Of course, as their history shows, it wasn't always easy. Groundwork had to be laid in order to establish this kind of success.

The Athletic Periods

IN THE STATE of Texas, programs are permitted to enroll their players in athletic periods year-round. Katy high school runs on a seven period day, leaving significantly less time for athletes than schools who have longer class periods. The way Katy is structured, the sophomores, juniors, and seniors participate in an athletic period during the fifth class of the day; the freshmen participate during the seventh class of the day. Twelve out of the thirteen coaches on the Katy staff have the two athletic periods as part of their teaching schedules; only one coach isn't present during athletic periods since he teaches at one of the middle schools.

Witnessing a fifty-minute athletic period with the older athletes serves as an example of efficiency; they all know how to get the most out of a short amount of time. When fourth period ends, an observer better watch where he/she stands in the field house because players literally come jogging in from their fourth period class. They then change quickly and head out to the field. Though one of the coaches hustles the players out, from the look of things, these athletes know the routine and really don't need prompting. If a couple of players are stragglers, they head onto the field where the captains already have the players in line for a short, organized three or four minute stretch. Without a coach's order, the consequence of being late drives the stragglers to immediately run up and down the field doing a summersault every ten yards. It is obvious that the Katy players hold each other accountable and demonstrate tremendous leadership and discipline.

Following the short stretch, the players break and run to their position coaches. Every athlete moves quickly to his assigned area where everyone will participate in position drills prior to reconvening for another session. Wide receivers and defensive backs compete against each other in one-on-ones while other position groups work on scheme installation. After a very competitive period, two huddles of offense go against two huddles of defense in a very fast-paced team session on each side of the field. At the conclusion of this period, players conclude practice by focusing on special teams or doing individual drills with their position groups. Overall, the Katy Tiger's athletic period is extremely impressive in terms of structure, discipline, and tempo. Even the athletic period practice sessions in the first week of April have the emotion and intensity of August preparation.

The 2007 Team

IN ROUTE TO an undefeated season, capped by a fifth state championship in Katy school history, the 2007 Tigers finished ranked fourth in the nation by *USA Today*. The offense averaged 43.8 points per game while the tenacious defense allowed only 8.1 points per game. Katy running back Aundre Dean, and quarterback Bo Levi Mitchell, were arguably as good of a one-two punch as any in the nation. Dean rushed for over twenty-four hundred yards despite missing one and one-half games with a broken hand. Mitchell had an unbelievable touchdown to interception ratio of 37:4. These statistics are even more impressive when one takes into account that rarely did either play deep into the third quarter throughout the season. Though this duo was phenomenal, they had a strong supporting cast as well. Seven players were signed to Division One scholarships from the 2007 team, and five more team, and five more signed scholarships to lower level schools. Dean signed to play at UCLA while Mitchell will join June Jones' pass-happy offense at Southern Methodist University in the fall of 2008. The 2007 team will go down as one of the best Katy teams to ever take the field.

The Memory

THE YEAR OF 2007 will be remembered in the Katy fans' minds as one exciting season. The Katy coaching staff will likely carry with it one of the most humorous sub-varsity game memories of their coaching careers. When the Katy junior varsity team was backed up to their own five-yard line, and forced to punt from their own end zone, one of the Katy assistants gave the punter the instruction to kick the ball out of the back of the end zone if the snap was bad; this was so that the team would sacrifice two points instead of seven in the event of a bad snap. The punter, who was a first-year football player and a lifelong soccer player, handled the punt well and got the punt away without a problem. Later in the game, Katy punted from midfield. This time, the snap was inaccurate and the punter quickly retrieved the ball and proceeded to launch a punt towards his *own* end zone. This permitted the punter to beat everyone to the ball. Then, with one final boot, the punter blasted the ball through his own end zone conceding two points to their opponent. Fortunate for Katy, this humorous event happened on the sub-varsity stage, and not during the varsity game. Had this transpired during a varsity game, many might have failed to see the humor.

The Facilities

THE FACILITIES AT Katy High School are very functional, but not extravagant. The Tigers share their stadium with at least four other schools in the district. Aside from their stadium, they have four grass practice fields—a necessity for the roughly three-hundred-fifty kids in the program. In 1997, a field house was added to the campus. The field house includes: a respectable weight room, coaches' offices, a team meeting room, a locker room, a training room, and general meeting rooms. Leading up to the field house, Tiger paw prints line the pavement giving the building an original feel before entering. Once inside, one notices that the booster club has decorated all of the walls with pictures of college players, photos from Katy games, and other inspirational traditions unique to Katy High School.

The Academic Standards

IN THE STATE of Texas, student athletes are held to very high academic standards. A player cannot be failing any classes in order to be eligible to participate in sports. This policy of *no pass no play* has never been felt as strongly as it was in the 1998 season at Katy High School. During 1998, the Katy Tigers went undefeated heading into the state playoffs. At the end of their quarterfinal game, they were leading 40-0; they began to play their backups. One of the players who saw minimal time at the conclusion of the game was the team's fourth string tight end. After the victory in the quarterfinals, Katy advanced to win their semi final game and set up a showdown with perennial power Midland Lee.

Midland Lee was led by future University of Texas and NFL star, Cedric Benson. The game was set to be a legendary showdown between two powerhouse schools. Katy had a good week of practice leading up to the state championship game, which was set to kickoff on a Saturday. The team boarded the bus to head to the state finals on Friday morning—the bus never left Katy. In the state quarterfinal victory, the fourth string tight end who played at the end of the game had forged his progress report without the knowledge of the Katy coaches. In fact, the coaches had the copy of the progress report that the player had forged.

In the team's semi-final game, the teacher of the student was in the stands and saw her student on the sideline suited up. She was confused as to why this athlete was ready to play in spite of a failing grade in her class. The team then, according to Texas rules, was forced to forfeit, permitting the semi-final opponent that Katy beat a week earlier a shot at the state championship. The team accepted the opportunity. However, having only one day of notice coupled with a lack of preparation, the game resulted in a lopsided victory for Midland Lee in the finals.

Texas Coaching Rules

WHILE MOST STATES are seeking as many volunteers as possible to help coach high school teams, the state of Texas holds unique requirements pertaining to being part of high school athletic programs. In the state of Texas, every high school football coach, volunteer or assistant, is required to be a school district employee. In the Katy Independent School District, the restrictions are even greater; they require all paid coaches to not only be employed by the school district, but serve in the role as a teacher within the district. This strict requirement clearly excludes paraprofessionals or classified staff from having the opportunities to coach. This policy benefits the program by ensuring that all of the coaches are working inside the school and around the players for many hours each day. Unfortunately, this policy also eliminates qualified coaches from being eligible if they don't work in the field of education. While many states would struggle to field complete coaching staffs with this policy, Texas football continues to thrive. It might even be argued that the players benefit from this policy since they have the advantage of being exposed to the consistency of coaches both in the classroom and on the football field.

South Panola High School

Batesville, Mississippi

Overview

AT THE OPENING of the 2008 football season the South Panoila Tigers start with the nation's longest active winning streak. This remarkable program has won the last five state championships amassing a 75-0 record along the way—this is in addition to state titles in 1993 and 1998. It is noteworthy that the last four head coaches have won state titles while coaching at South Panola.

During the last five seasons, the South Panola Tigers have concluded each season by being ranked in the top ten of the nation, according to *USA Today*. Batesville, Mississippi, home to the South Panola Tigers, is a primarily blue-collar community where the football team reflects the community at large. It would be fair to assess the football team as a rough and tough blue-collar team.

Head Coach Lance Pogue, who just finished his first year at South Panola, says that most of his players don't own cars, but are bused to school. Coach Pogue believes that football means more to the players on his team than it does to most other schools.

With a school population around thirteen hundred, South Panola is small in comparison to other public school powerhouses across the nation. This enrollment size establishes them near the middle of the pack of the thirty-two large classification schools in Mississippi. Each home game draws between seven and eight thousand fans.

In Mississippi, many athletes have opportunities to play after high school because Mississippi is a big junior college state when it comes to football. There are six junior colleges in the northern part of the state, and six junior colleges in the southern part of the state that have football programs. These twelve junior colleges grant scholarships for football and are all very competitive.

In a program where the offensive line coach doubles as an arena league football player, athletes are inspired to dream of playing at the next level. The aspiration to play college football generally begins early in life when young kids play youth football in Batesville, Mississippi. Spring football, which typically begins at the high school level, starts as early as the elementary school level with the youth football program in Batesville. South Panola High School and the town of Batesville have placed themselves on the national map of high school football with their successful five-year run; the players and coaches seek even bigger things in the future.

The Off-season

SOUTH PANOLA HIGH School is set on a seven period class schedule. The freshmen join each other for an athletic period during the fifth class of the day. The rest of the athletes in the program have two athletic periods during the sixth and seventh hours of the school day. The entire coaching staff, which amounts to nine assistant coaches and the head coach, each has fifth, sixth, and seventh periods together as part of their teaching schedule.

Nearly 50 freshmen participate in the fifth period class, and approximately 90 varsity members participate in the last two athletic periods. The rules in Mississippi permit teams to practice football without pads *or* lifting during the year-round athletic periods. While the workout schedule consists of two upper body workouts and two lower body workouts per week, Head Coach Lance Pogue is direct in stating that South Panola's strength program isn't the secret to their success. Pogue believes that the talent level at South Panola High is a big contributor to the success of the program. The highly talented athletes of South Panola, blended with a program that has a deep playbook on both sides of the football, makes up their formula for success. It is worth mentioning that the playbook is executed at a high level because of the amount of time the entire coaching staff dedicates to players year-round.

Coach Pogue believes that the work ethic of his players exemplifies superiority. He also thinks that his players outwork athletes from other programs. While the coaching staff has minimal trouble training players during the school day, summer workouts can prove a bit more difficult. One incentive to attend summer workouts comes through the implementation of a reward-based system. If players want their names on the back of their jerseys, they have to earn that privilege; they must attend a set number of summer workouts for this to happen.

The Foundation of Strength

WHILE THE WEIGHT room consists of four bench press stations, four incline press stations, four military press units, four leg curl stations, and five squat racks, it is very basic. South Panola's weight room is not flashy or state-of-the-art, but it is very functional and practical. The functionality and practicality of this weight room can be seen in the overall strength of the players. The 2007 team contained: over twelve players who bench pressed at least three hundred pounds, and twenty-five who squatted at least four hundred pounds. Part of this strength success can be attributed to the low coach to player workout ratio.

When watching the South Panola freshmen go through an off-season workout in the weight room, it becomes clear that the South Panola Tigers are much stronger than most other schools. The majority of the fifty freshmen can squat over three hundred pounds with some already over four hundred pounds; one is close to five hundred pounds. The majority of the freshmen can perform multiple reps at two hundred twenty-five pounds on the bench press, with a few players nearing a three hundred pound maximum. According to the coaches at South Panola, twenty-eight out of fifty freshmen were clocked at 4.8 seconds or faster in the forty-yard dash. Also apparent in the workout were the strong discipline and work ethics of the players. It is observable that players come to attention quickly when a coach gives direction—the players are dedicated and ready to work.

Many athletes in the South Panola football program begin their football training with the high school team the summer before their ninth grade year; this gives them a head start on the season. Each of the two middle schools feeding into South Panola High School has its own weight program, thus enabling players to begin lifting weights and training in seventh grade. Judging by the graduating class of 2011, South Panola football is not projected to slow down in its dominance of Mississippi high school football.

The Program

WHEN SPEAKING WITH Head Coach Lance Pogue about what is needed to build a successful program, his first response is talented players—South Panola has just that. The second ingredient that Coach Pogue looks for is players with strong work ethics. Thirdly,

Courtesy pso.com

Colerain takes the field against rival, St. Xavier.

Courtesy pso.com

Colerain teammates celebrate another Cardinal score.

Kralik

Inside the weight room at Colerain, a clock counts down the time until the 2008 opener with St. Xavier.

Kralik

Christmas is the only day the Colerain Cardinals get off from their four day per week lifting schedule.

Kralik

The weight room at Colerain is where the Cardinals make up for not having spring football.

Alex Rowell

An overhead look at a recent Lowndes home game against rival, Valdosta High School.

Al Rowell

The Lowndes offense executing their famous off tackle play in the Georgia Dome.

Al Rowell

The success of the Lowndes football program is built around a physical defense that runs to the football well.

Al Rowell

Coach McPherson leads his program onto the field at a recent home game.

Kralik

A look at the main entrance to Lowndes High School.

Alex Rowell

The 5,000 square football weight room at Lowndes
was completed in July of 2008.

Alex Rowell

The Lowndes Stadium which is nicknamed the Concrete Palace
installed field turf for the 2008 season.

Alex Rowell

The Lowndes Vikings will run down this newly installed ramp to take the field in 2008.

Tim Eddington

A picture from the 2004 Louisiana State Championship game between Evangel and West Monroe (Louisiana).

Tim Eddington

Jacob Hester carrying the ball for Evangel at a home game against Rock Hurst (Missouri).

Tim Eddington

Jacob Hester leaping into the endzone against Alabama.

Tim Eddington

A game against Abiline Christian at Texas Stadium shows the innovative 9 yard shotgun by Evangel.

Tim Eddington

Evangel trying to defend Tony Temple, who went on to have a great career at the University of Missouri.

Kralik

A look at the *home* side of the Evangel Stadium.

Kralik

The *visitor* side of the stadium at Evangel High School.

Kralik

The scoreboard at Evangel reminds fans of how fast Evangel football has risen to national stardom.

Kralik

The weight room at Evangel will soon be replaced by a facility that will be able to train 100 athletes at a time.

Courtesy pso.com

The De La Salle Spartans taking the field at the 2007 Ohio vs. The Nation Classic in Ohio.

Bob Sansoe

Maurice Jones-Drew before one of his games as a De La Salle Spartan.

Bob Sansoe

Maurice Jones-Drew taking the field in Hawaii against St. Louis High School.

Bob Sansoe

The De La Salle Spartans getting ready to play Bellevue (WA) at Quest Field in 2004.

Bob Sansoe

De La Salle against Bellevue (WA) in 2004 when the 151 game winning streak came to an end.

Bob Sansoe

De La Salle Head Coach Bob Ladouceur will begin his thirtieth season as Head Coach of De La Salle in 2008.

Kralik

A look at the *home* side of the De La Salle Stadium.

Kralik

A look at the courtyard area at De La Salle High School.

Kralik

De La Salle Head Coach Bob Ladouceur would put his team up against any in terms of physical strength.

Kralik

De La Salle Head Coach Bob Ladouceur believes the demanding off season program is the team's number one team builder.

Kralik

A sign in the De La Salle lockeroom runs much deeper than a nice slogan at De La Salle.

Courtesy pso.com

The Independence Patriots take the field at a recent home game.

Courtesy pso.com

The 109 game winning streak came to an end as Elder (Ohio) defeated Independence at the Ohio vs. The Nation Classic in 2007.

Courtesy pso.com

Independence won seven consecutive large classifications State Championships in North Carolina.

Kralik

The weight room at Independence is a place where strong work ethics are formed.

Kralik

The Independence players lift five days a week both in season and out of season.

University of Florida

Chris Leak led Independence to three State Championships before leading the University of Florida to a National Championship in 2007.

Mary Sharp

The Jenks Trojans take the field at a recent game. Jenks has won nine of the last twelve 6A State Championships in Oklahoma.

Mary Sharp

The Jenks vs. Union rivalry is arguably the best high school football rivalry in nation.

Kralik

A look at the home side of the Jenks Stadium.

Kralik

The high school football facility of all facilities resides on the campus of Jenks High School.

Kralik

A look at the third floor of Jenks facility is home to a large team banquet room with coaches offices in the background.

Kralik

When one gets off of the elevator at the Robert L. Sharp Center, this is what is seen at Jenks.

Kralik

The Jenks weight room has over twenty multi-purpose training stations in it.

Kralik

The weight room at Jenks is close to 5,000 square feet.

Kralik

The second floor of the Robert L. Sharp Fitness Center is home to a fitness center in addition to the weight room on the first floor.

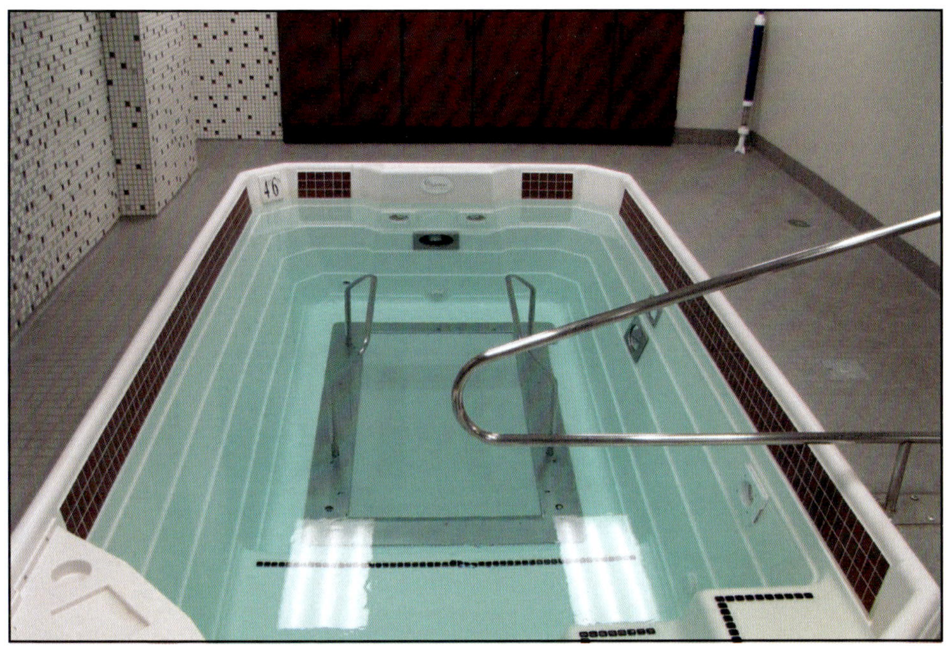

Kralik

The training room at Jenks has the $50,000 hydrotherapy pool with a treadmill that goes up to seven miles per hour.

Kralik

The Robert L. Sharp Fitness Center has multiple large meeting rooms where players and coaches split up for film sessions.

R.E.B. Photo

The Carroll Dragons take the field at a 2007 home game.

R.E.B. Photo

The Dragons celebrate a one point victory against Euless Trinity during the 2006 playoffs in front of close to 50,000 fans.

R.E.B. Photo

Carroll Head Coach Hal Wasson says the number one prerequisite for being a Carroll Dragon is being 100% unselfish.

Kralik

A look at the home side of Dragon Stadium in Southlake, Texas.

Kralik

Season ticket holders are the only ones assured seats at Carroll Dragon football games.

Kralik

A look at the outside of the Carroll Dragons' football stadium which has its own store inside that is open year round.

Kralik

The indoor football facility at Carroll High School has been been borrowed by the Dallas Cowboys on occasion.

Kralik

The Carroll Dragons lift either two days a week or three days a week during the off season.

R.E.B. Photo

The 2007 game between Miami Northwestern and Carroll matched the top teams from the states of Texas and Florida.

R.E.B. Photo

The Miami Northwestern captains meet the Carroll captains in the center of a sold out stadium on the campus of SMU.

Courtesy pso.com

The Katy Tigers take the field with a confidence that is built on a rich tradition of success.

Courtesy pso.com

The Katy Tigers prepare for the 2007 State Championship game in the Alamo Dome.

Kralik

The Katy Tigers share their stadium with other schools in their school district.

Kralik

Katy has advanced to at least the state quarterfinal round of the playoffs nine of the last ten years.

Kralik

Tickets to see Katy games have been as cheap as $4 since the 1980's.

Kralik

Head Coach Gary Joseph addressing his team after a workout during one of the athletic periods. The Katy weight room is in the background.

Kralik

The Katy Tigers have a strong work ethic that is developed in the weight room as well as other places.

Kralik

The Katy players will either lift weights during the athletic period or after school.

Kralik

The trophy case at Katy displays the rich tradition of Katy football.

Courtesy pso.com

In Batesville, Mississippi, South Panola football is the hottest ticket in town.

Courtesy pso.com

The South Panola Tigers enter the 2008 football season with the longest high school winning streak in the nation.

Kralik

A look at the *home* side of Tiger Stadium on the campus of South Panola High School.

Kralik

The football stadium is one of the nicest amenities of the South Panola football program.

Kralik

A look at the scoreboard in one of the end zones at South Panola.

Kralik

The weight room at South Panola is very average at best; it shows that dynasties can be built without glamorous facilities.

Kralik

Central Catholic High School is located in a busy section of Pittsburgh right across the street from the University of Pittsburgh.

Kralik

The jersey of Hall of Fame quarterback and Central Catholic alumnus, Dan Marino, hangs on the wall of the weight room.

Kralik

The Central Catholic Vikings play a physical brand of football that is developed in the weight room.

Kralik

Central Catholic averages around sixty players at each of their after school workouts.

Kralik

The single practice field at Central Catholic must be shared by the entire program.

Michael Wilson / The Ledger

The Lakeland team takes the field with the $400,000 scoreboard in the background.

Kralik

The *home* side of the Lakeland Stadium.

Kralik

The *visitor* side of the Lakeland Dreadnaught Stadium.

Kralik

The Team Meeting Room for the Lakeland Dreadnaughts;
NFL jerseys on the back wall.

Kralik

In the team meeting room, pictures of all the Dreadnaughts that went on to play Division One Football hang on the wall.

Kralik

The Lakeland weight room is around 2,000 square feet, but the floor space is utilized very efficiently.

Kralik

Each training station has everything needed to complete the entire workout without having to leave the station.

Kralik

Lakeland players are reminded daily that they are part of something bigger than themselves.

Ildiko Matchus

The Miami Northwestern Bulls take the field at a recent home game.

Ildiko Matchus

The eight seniors from the 2007 team who signed scholarships with the University of Miami together making the famous 'U" sign.

Ildiko Matchus

The 2007 team is sent off to Orlando to play for the State Championship.

Ildiko Matchus

The Boone High School (Florida) crowd hoped for an upset in the State Championship Game.

Ildiko Matchus

The Bulls prepare to take the field for the 2007 State Championship game.

Ildiko Matchus

The Miami Northwestern captains head out for the coin toss before the state finals.

Ildiko Matchus

Miami Northwestern in their "difficult to defend" spread offense.

Kralik

The weight room at Miami Northwestern, where future Division One players are developed.

Coach Pogue believes a program needs to have solid coaching. Lastly, Pogue is convinced that a program needs a coaching staff, administrative staff, and a community who are united through a shared vision. Coach Pogue believes that the culmination of these four factors establishes the foundation for something special to take root.

South Panola is located within a community that is very supportive of its football program. Residents in Batesville, Mississippi, appear to take great pride in their town. Part of that pride trickles down to the football program where the community sets the bar high and expects the Tigers to win their football games. The community supports the program financially with a booster club that raises roughly sixty thousand dollars a year.

The administrative support at South Panola High School is also extremely high. While a lack of administrative support often frustrates some coaches, Head Coach Lance Pogue couldn't praise his administrative staff enough. Two examples of administrative support are illustrated in the provision for athletic periods during the school days, and the manner in which they have historically handled the transitions of outgoing and incoming head coaches.

While some of the programs in Mississippi do not have athletic periods during their school day, and are then at disadvantages to the schools that do, South Panola is not only granted one athletic period per day, but three. Pogue states that the administration he works for places a high priority on athletics, and understands the significance of football in the development of athletes' lives.

In March of 2008, when Pogue was hired to replace the previous head coach who left to take another job, the administration provided the program with a strong transition period. Coach Pogue, who came from another program, was immediately given a job working on campus at South Panola; one of his assistant coaches was hired on campus at the same time as well. The administrative staff allowed them to begin working with the athletes, and incorporating program-building immediately. This smooth transition contributed to the program finishing yet another undefeated season capped off by its fifth consecutive state championship.

The Streak

WITH THE LONGEST active high school football winning streak, the South Panola Tigers have developed a program that has gained national attention. During the past few years, the streak has gained notoriety. With Independence High School (North Carolina) having their winning streak snapped at 109 games in 2007, the South Panola Tigers are the next team with a shot at breaking the historical 151 game winning streak record achieved by De La Salle High School (California) between 1992 and 2004. South Panola, like Independence High School, managed to change head coaches in the middle of the streak and still maintain it. South Panola sustained the winning streak after hiring a replacement head coach from outside of the current coaching staff; Independence did it by promoting an assistant from within their program.

During the last three years, South Panola has played five games outside of the state of Mississippi, and won all five. Each of the five out-of-state opponents was from the bordering state of Tennessee. Many high school football enthusiasts would love to see South Panola put their streak on the line against opponents from a top tier high school football state such as: Texas, Florida, California, Ohio, or Pennsylvania. In 2008, the enthusiasts will get their wish, as the Tigers of South Panola play host to a top tier team from Florida, Apopka High School. Apopka is a 6A program just coming off of a 12-2 season with a three point playoff loss to the eventual state runner-up, Boone High School. The South Panola vs. Apopka showdown is projected to gain national attention as the game approaches. There has also been talk of South Panola playing De La Salle (California) in the future if the Tigers can preserve their winning streak. The Tigers, now at 75 consecutive victories, are still only half way to the 151 consecutive victories that De La Salle put up.

The Facilities

IF THERE EVER is a school that proves that nice, state of the art facilities are not a prerequisite to building a top tier high school football program on a national level, it is South Panola. While the high school building is remarkable, the football facilities are not consistent with the rest of the school's campus. The football field house is a metal pole building that houses: the weight room, a couple of meeting rooms, junior varsity and varsity locker rooms, an equipment room, a laundry facility, and a training room. Though the program has all the things needed in one location, the makeup of all of the facilities within the field house are adequate at best. From a facility standpoint, the stadium is the nicest thing the Tigers' football program has. The stands are usually full, and a typical home game brings in around sixty thousand dollars to the school.

Recruiting

THE MOST NOTABLE alumni from the South Panola football program are two members of the 1993 State Championship team. Deshea Townsend was a standout player at the University of Alabama prior to contributing to the recent Pittsburgh Steelers Super Bowl 40 victory in 2006. Dwayne Rudd, who played with Townsend at South Panola and later at the University of Alabama, was a first-round draft choice of the Minnesota Vikings in 1997.

The 2007 South Panola football team produced 15 athletes who signed football scholarships; five of them signed with Division One programs. During the past seven seasons, the Tigers have sent 18 players to Division One programs. Most of these players stayed in stayed in state with seven heading to the University of Mississippi, and four more attending Southern Mississippi University.

High School Football in Mississippi

IN THE STATE of Mississippi, teams are allowed fifteen days for spring football. Ten of the fifteen days can be in pads, while the other five must be in shorts. One of the fifteen days of football can be a scrimmage or a jamboree against other schools. Athletic periods are also permitted in Mississippi, and South Panola makes the best use of this by having three total athletic periods. Teams are permitted to work on football related activities during the athletic period as long as it doesn't extend beyond the school day.

In the off-season, when the school days are finished for the summer, all football-related activities must cease in accordance with Mississippi rules. Unlike many other top programs, South Panola does not hold two-a-day practices in the fall. With school starting earlier than many places, scheduling many two-a-days proves difficult. Aside from the logistical difficulty, Head Coach Lance Pogue opts out of two-a-days with the purpose of ensuring that his players and coaches are fresh heading into the long season that South Panola plays each year, including their traditional playoff runs. The Tigers have played as many as sixteen games throughout the course of a single season, and at South Panola, the long season is something both planned for and expected. The South Panola Tigers are truly a program that expects to play for state titles each year, because they have the program in place to do so.

Central Catholic High School

Pittsburgh, Pennsylvania

Overview

WITH AN ALUMNUS pedigree that includes Dan Marino and Trent Bulger, Central Catholic High School, located in Pittsburgh, Pennsylvania, stands as one of the most prestigious schools and includes one of the most respected football programs in the entire state of Pennsylvania. Pennsylvania is a state that maintains a reputation for its spirit and toughness in life and in the sport of football; the Central Catholic Vikings contribute to this reputation.

The appeal of Central Catholic High School is so strong, that some of its students will commute more than eighty miles round-trip each school day to be a part of this legacy. The strong impact of this high school lingers in its alumni long after graduation. Many elite high schools across the country cannot compete with the loyalty that Central Catholic alumni continue to show years after they graduate. To draw ten thousand fans at a single game is not uncommon for this powerful team. However, a more remarkable illustration of this loyalty and passion is displayed in the loyalty of the Viking's football staff in that it is primarily made up of Central Catholic Alumni.

Even though Head Coach Terry Totten says that most high school programs can be run well with only three coaches, Central Catholic's football program employs twenty coaches on staff for the benefit of their program. It becomes very clear right away that these coaches are not in it for the money; the entire coaching staff voluntarily divides a total of four coaching stipends amongst all twenty coaches. When the drive of money is eliminated from the picture, what is left is a team of coaches who are choosing to be there for the betterment of the team. This mentality is why Coach Totten finds it very difficult to turn down skilled people who want to help with the football program and give back to the school that gave so much to them.

The Program

MOST HIGH SCHOOLS would jump at the chance to employ a coach who had sixteen years of college coaching experience, ten of them being at Division 1AA schools, part of that as a Defensive Coordinator. Fortunately for Pittsburgh's Central Catholic High School, this impressive résumé, coupled with a passion for Central Catholic's football program, accompanied Head Coach Terry Totten when he began coaching at Central Catholic.

Like all of the males in his family, Totten attended and graduated from Central Catholic High School; he was part of the class of 1976. Before joining the Viking coaching staff as the Defensive Coordinator in 2001, Central Catholic held a record of 15-16 over the three previous seasons. During the past seven seasons since Totten's arrival in 2001, Central Catholic achieved an impressive record of 83-11.

Focusing more specifically on the last four seasons (2004-2007), the Vikings accomplished a record of 53-4 with two 4A state titles. Central Catholic finished 6th in the nation in 2004 and 11th in the nation in 2007, according to the USA Today nationwide prep poll. In 2008, the Vikings are set to travel to West Virginia to play Lakeland High School. The national implication of this type of prestigious game is a huge driving force in the season-long preparation seen in the Vikings.

The Staff

WITH TWENTY COACHES on staff, Central Catholic's staff is large, even by today's standards. Out of these twenty football coaches, only two are employed in the high school building. One coach serves as the Dean of Students, and Head Coach Terry Totten recently started a job working in the weight room. The combined total profit of Totten's two positions is a meager $12,000 a year; the assistant coaches make significantly less. Even with the very limited amount of money the assistant coaches earn, one will find five or six coaches working with around sixty players in the weight room on any given day during the off-season.

With an estimated one-third of the football team coming from single-parent homes, it seems that the coaches understand they have greater purposes with their players than just coaching football. Coaches involve themselves with many facets of players' lives. Examples of this include the way the coaches hold the players and each other accountable for using clean language on and off the field. Additionally, the players at Central Catholic are held to higher athletic eligibility requirements than the public schools require in Pennsylvania.

Like most quality programs, Central Catholic football is structured around a team concept; Coach Totten doesn't emphasize the individual. Coach Totten reiterates to his team that when players are interviewed following Super Bowl victories, they acknowledge how much they value their teammates. He emphasizes the idea that successful teams are ones that build family environments and generate enjoyment for those who compose them.

When hiring coaches, Coach Totten says that he looks for coaches with the student athletes' best interests at heart. Fundamental to Totten's coaching mission is that along the way to winning state championships and competing on a national level, Central Catholic coaches strive to provide players with healthy foundations that will serve them well throughout the rest of their lives.

The School

CENTRAL CATHOLIC HIGH School was founded in 1927 as a Roman Catholic school for boys. Originally, there were four hundred eighty-eight freshmen who were members of forty-two local Catholic parishes. After reaching an enrollment level of over eighteen hundred students in the 1950s, class sizes had increased to approximately forty-five students; it didn't take long to realize that there was a problem at hand. Because of this overcrowding dilemma, concentrated efforts were made to reduce class sizes. Today, around nine hundred students make up the student enrollment; the average class size is around twenty-one.

There are a few other notable aspects of Central Catholic that set the school apart from other area schools. First, as a private school, there is a seven thousand dollar annual tuition cost per student. Next, a strict dress code is required of all students in attendance. Also, the academic rigor of the institution requires that students keep their grade point averages above seventy percent in each class in order to receive a passing grade.

Central Catholic High School is located directly across from the University of Pittsburgh. This location is in a very busy portion of town where buildings rest snugly on each side of the school building. When looking more specifically at the Viking's football facilities, they could be considered average in comparison to many of the programs they compete against. First, Central Catholic's football program only has one practice field; all one hundred-fifty players must share this field at the same time. Also, while the weight room is functional, it is only around two-thousand square feet. Finally, the football program does not have its own stadium and plays home games at various sites. It seems that what the football program lacks in impressive facilities, it makes up for in coaching staff. This is illustrated by the fact that there have only been three head coaches at the school in the past twenty-six years. Also, since so many successful alumni are still connected to the school through coaching, these players often have great support when seeking employment opportunities throughout the city of Pittsburgh.

The Alumni

WHEN ONE ENTERS the Central Catholic High School weight room, their eyes are immediately drawn to the professional jerseys of Dan Marino and Trent Bulger, which are displayed on the wall. Because of the notoriety of these two players, it is easy to overlook the impressive fact that the current starting fullback for the Minnesota Vikings, Jeff Dugan, is also a Central Catholic graduate. In all, approximately ninety players since 1950 have gone on from Central Catholic to receive scholarships to Division One schools. In 2007, the senior class produced five Division One players and three more Division 1AA players. Additionally, Central Catholic has been well represented in the Big 33 game since its start in 1957; it has contributed around forty-five players to the game throughout the years.

The Program

WHEN EXAMINING CENTRAL Catholic High School, it is interesting to note that the football players do not train during the school day as part of physical education classes. Unlike most programs that begin teaching the incoming players how to perform core lifts (bench presses, squats, power cleans, and dead lifts, etc.), Central Catholic takes a different approach. The Viking coaches' perspective is that they first need to develop the incoming players through supplemental lifts prior to starting the core lift training. The coaches initially put the younger players through a completely different program from the older players.

Throughout the year, there is an average of sixty players present for workouts at any given time; a ratio of one coach for every ten players is standard for each of the workouts. Because the small weight room is unable to safely handle all sixty players, the athletes are split up during the workouts. The workouts each take nearly ninety minutes; this timeframe ensures that players are rotated between training exercises inside the small weight room and exercises out on the practice field. Outside on the practice field, the workout concentrates on speed, agility, and plyometric drills.

A more specified core principle in Central Catholic's strength program is that the coaching staff targets ten top linemen per year as their highest priority. While the rest of the team is encouraged to participate in multiple sports— these ten linemen, however, are assessed very carefully. Whether or not these ten athletes will benefit more from another sport or training in the weight room during the off-season, is considered very thoroughly by the coaching staff before recommendations are given as to each athlete as to whether he should participate in other sports or focus on the specific training needed for football.

The Philosophy

WHEN TALKING WITH Head Coach Terry Totten, it doesn't take long to discover that he's a down-to-earth straight-shooter with some very remarkable thoughts about building a successful high school football program. Even though he brings a wealth of knowledge to his program from his time spent coordinating at the college level, his focus at Central Catholic is doing a few things *really* well on offense and on defense.

On offense, the Vikings are a team heavy on two back sets; they also run the football seventy percent of the time. Within their running game, they have four to five base running plays that are foundational and take up the bulk of their teaching time. On the defense, they are a base 4-4 Cover 3 team. Although this seems almost as basic as possible, Coach Totten emphasizes that he truly believes in being an eight-man-front team at the high school level. His strategy here is to play an eight-man-front until their opponent forces them out of it.

Coach Totten clearly outlines three things that they won't do. The first is that the staff does not grade game film. He believes that this is a waste of time because they already know who their players are. The second thing is that they do not give individual awards out, such as helmet stickers, because he believes this is a waste of valuable time. Lastly, they do not breakdown their opponents by down and distance, and plays run on specific hashes. This is because Coach Totten believes that high school football is a formation game; therefore, when studying opponents, it is beneficial to approach scouting from the angle of determining what plays are run from each formation.

In accordance with Coach Totten's philosophy, the only time that Central Catholic films practice is during two-a-days in August. This is done out of the end zone with the primary focus on teaching offensive line play. The Viking's approach is unique when it comes to contact in practice. Although one of the goals in practice is to keep the players injury-free, the Vikings do practice some live plays between the number one offense and number one defense throughout the season twice a week.

Another unique perspective from Coach Totten is that he is adamant about the necessity of respect over being liked. He says that having respect is critical when dealing with the younger players entering the program. Because of this approach, his staff is very focused on commanding the respect of the players without putting their focus on being liked by them.

When it comes to hiring coaches, Coach Totten is clear about the three things he looks for in the respective order. First, he wants absolute loyalty to the head coach and the program. Second, he only hires coaches with solid character because this is what they are trying to instill in the players. Coach Totten sees his coaching staff as the role models of this. Third, he wants all coaches to have the kids' best interests at heart and not choose to coach as a way of living vicariously through the players. Coach Totten states that it is much easier to find coaches to merely teach football to players than it is find coaches who are willing to teach football *and* possess the above three characteristics. He also adds that it is a huge asset to have a coach who has the desired characteristics *and* brings a high level of intelligence to the field. Coach Totten is a perfect example of somebody who has a clear strategy of what he deems important in his coaching philosophy. He doesn't just speak these things—he lives them.

The Big 33 Football Classic

TO UNDERSTAND THE history of high school football one must understand the significance of the Big 33 Game. The Big 33 Football Classic is truly the most prestigious high school all-star game that impacts the participants far beyond the football field. What has been described by many as the *Super Bowl of High School Football,* it is much more than a typical high school all-star game. The game was founded in 1957, however, in the past 16 years it has become an exclusive contest between the top 33 Pennsylvania high school players and the top 33 high school players from Ohio.

After the match-up in 2008, Pennsylvania led the series 9-7; the seventeenth match-up is set for June of 2009. Prior to the Pennsylvania and Ohio rivalry, some opponents of the Pennsylvania all-stars included Maryland and Texas players. An amazing statistic is that every Super Bowl since the start of the Big 33 has involved at least one Big 33 alumnus playing. Some of the NFL alumni who have played in this event include: Tony Dorsett, Matt Millen, Joe Montana, Joe Namath, John Cappelletti, Dan Marino, Jim Kelly, Rocket Ismail, Kerry Collins, Kyle Brady, Orlando Pace, Ricky Watters, Antonio Freeman, Ed McCaffrey, Marvin Harrison, Sean Gilbert, Curtis Martin, and Ben Roethlisberger.

The Big 33 event is much more than a showcase of great talent. Since 1985, this event has raised over 3 million dollars for academic scholarships. There is also a unique facet to this event called the *Buddy Program.* This program matches every player with a youth who has exceptional needs. These matches share meals together, attend the banquet together, and go through the game introductions together. Also, players do not stay in dorms during the Big 33 week. Rather, players lodge with host families in order to create another layer of memories to take away from this exceptional event. It would be fair to say that the Big 33 Football Classic impacts lives through camaraderie, scholarships, and stardom long after the game has been played.

Lakeland High School

Lakeland, Florida

Overview

DESPITE THE MAJORITY of Florida attracting multitudes of people in their retirement, the city of Lakeland does not fit this trend. Located precisely one hour west of Orlando, Lakeland is a community that has enjoyed rich success on the gridiron since the arrival of Head Coach Bill Castle thirty-two years ago.

The Lakeland Football Program has won three of the past four 5A State Championships in Florida; they have claimed six State Championships since 1986. In addition, the Lakeland Dreadnaughts finished number one in the nation in 2005, and third in 2006 according to *USA Today*. In 2006, Lakeland finished first in the nation according to two separate polls—they had earned the prestigious title for two consecutive years. Initially, the Dreadnaughts began this run with a top twenty finish in 2004 according to the *USA Today* national poll.

The Lakeland program has not had a losing season since Head Coach Castle took over the head coaching job in 1976. Friday nights create an electric event that averages nearly fifty-five hundred fans. A Jumbo-Tron, purchased by the booster club for four hundred thousand dollars sits in one end zone and adds to the thrill of the Friday night experience. On the home side of the stadium, during a game, one will find a large Dreadnaught battleship and a twelve hundred pound bell that rings throughout each game.

Lakeland is a program that not only plays the best of Florida, but also travels outside of their state to compete against top teams around the nation. In 2006, Lakeland journeyed up to Ohio to square off with St. Xavier High School—they walked away with a three point victory in overtime. To open the season in 2008, the Dreadnaughts travel to West Virginia to take on Pittsburgh's Central Catholic. It is clear when studying the football program at Lakeland High School that the strength program, coaching stability, and community support are the top three facets of their success.

The Program

LAKELAND HIGH SCHOOL is a ninth through twelfth grade high school. The football program is split into two separate programs, the junior varsity and varsity. In Polk County, home of the Lakeland Dreadnaughts, there are not separate ninth grade programs like elsewhere in the country. The ninth graders are simply combined with some tenth and eleventh grade athletes to create the ninety junior varsity players; the varsity team is composed of approximately sixty-five players.

The coaching staff is split down the middle, contributing eight coaches to the varsity team, and eight coaches to the junior varsity team. The junior varsity staff is composed of two paid coaches and six volunteers. One of the challenges that Lakeland faces is that there are only eight junior varsity games per season. It often becomes very challenging to maintain interest in football for the freshmen players without separate ninth grade games. This is because many freshmen are given so little playing time when there are sophomores and juniors on their junior varsity team as well.

Coach Castle admits that when Lakeland transitioned from a tenth through twelfth grade school to a ninth through twelfth grade school, it became increasingly difficult to retain players throughout their high school years if they were not key contributors to the program early on. Athletes who could make an impact on the varsity program as juniors and seniors would frequently drop out before getting to that point. Another challenge that Lakeland currently faces is that they do not have a single middle school that fully feeds into them. The middle schools in Polk County are split up amongst several high schools.

The Strength Program

ONE OF THE key ingredients to Lakeland Football success is their strength and conditioning program. The weight room, standing at barely over two thousand square feet is small. However, the team workouts are efficiently designed to maximize a smooth-running regime without wasting time or space. The layout of the weight room consists of five multi-purpose racks on each side for a combined total of ten. Each multi-purpose station includes: a full rack, an adjustable bench, a platform, and a set of dumbbells. Each station also contains its own weights attached to the full rack and a set of bumper plates located underneath the dumbbell racks. This might seem an insignificant point until one observes a team workout.

Lakeland High School has four, ninety minute classes each day. One assistant coach is responsible for training thirty players at a time. For each workout, three athletes are grouped at each of the ten stations. The pace of the workout is rapid and intense. As soon as the first player concludes his set, the next athlete in his group is ready to go at the command of the coach's whistle. By using this method of training, they are able to cut the rest periods down and complete significantly more sets than other programs. This is also partly because of the ninety minute class periods.

The time spent switching weights is minimal because each station has its own set of weights, bumper plates, and dumbbells. This is beneficial in that players do not have to move away from their stations in order to retrieve the weights for the next person to lift. The stamina and recovery rate of the players participating in this workout appear to be compare favorably to other typical high school workouts, providing an advantage to these players. With each group performing the same lift or exercise simultaneously, it is easier for only one coach to monitor the entire workout while each athlete is held accountable for completing every set and repetition.

Data collection is another key component within the strength and conditioning program. Players are periodically tested, and the results are then entered into the computer. Player improvements can easily be tracked and teams can be compared to each other as a result of compiling this data. For example, the 2005 Dreadnaughts finished first in the nation according to *USA Today,* and was one of the best teams in the weight room, as well as on the field. The 2005 team had: nine players who could squat over four hundred pounds, thirty-four players who could squat over three hundred fifteen pounds, twenty-three players who could power clean over two hundred twenty-five pounds, forty-seven players who could power clean over two hundred pounds, and seventeen players who could bench press at least three hundred pounds. Coach Castle stresses that there is a definite correlation between the physical strength of their teams and the successes on the field. More often than not, the stronger teams produce state championships while the teams that don't measure up in strength usually exit the playoffs sooner than they would like.

The Coaches

HEAD COACH BILL Castle first began coaching at Lakeland High School in 1971. Back then, he started out as an assistant coach to Head Coach Paul Quinn. In 1976, Quinn left Lakeland for another job. Castle didn't intend to apply for the head coaching job until people at Lakeland urged him in that direction. Since taking over as head coach in 1976, Castle has never produced a losing season; he has amassed a career record of 312-74 to accompany six state titles.

Coach Castle has coached many of his current players' dads throughout his tenure at Lakeland. Athletes entering the Lakeland program generally have a good grasp of what to expect; this does not change from the time that they enter as freshman and exit as seniors. The consistency of Coach Castle has permeated the entire coaching staff. Most coaches agree that the longer an entire staff is together, the more efficiently they will work. The Lakeland football program is one of the top models to support this theory. At one point, Coach Castle had four assistant coaches on his staff who had been assisting under him for over twenty years. In an era when high school coaches often mirror the college coaching scene, with coaches making several moves throughout their careers, Lakeland High School has produced unparalleled stability within their coaching staff. This consistency contributes to the teams' dominance on the field.

The Dreadnaughts

LAKELAND HIGH SCHOOL may be the only school in the nation that has a Dreadnaught as a mascot. The story of how Lakeland became the home of the Dreadnaughts stretches back eighty years—it is an important part of Lakeland football. To understand significance of this mascot, one must first learn what it is. Initially, the first dreadnaught was called a dreadnought; a dreadnought was an "all big gun" elitist battleship used in its day.

In 1923, Lakeland High School went undefeated in their football season that year. It was at the end of this accomplishment that Principal I.G. McKay addressed the student body at an assembly. As he closed his speech, the legendary McKay compared the football team to the mighty dreadnaught because of how they rolled over their opponents just as the military dreadnaught rolled through the seas. McKay then went on to suggest that the team should be forever known as the Lakeland Dreadnaughts—a name that has stuck for the past 86 years.

Recruiting

AS COACH CASTLE states, "recruiting comes in waves," meaning some years there are plenty of prospects, while other years there are very few prospects. If this holds true, 2006 was a title wave for Lakeland recruiting. In this one recruiting class, seven players signed scholarships with the University of Florida, one player signed with Louisiana State University, and one signed with the University Alabama. Based on the seven 2006 players signing with Florida, one might conclude that there is a strong connection between the University of Florida and Lakeland High School. Prior to 2006, the last player to sign with the University of Florida was in 1983.

After leaving Lakeland, athlete Wayne Peace became a four-year starter, as quarterback, for the University of Florida. Lakeland maintains a strong legacy for players going on to major colleges, and NFL careers as well. David Williams started for four years at the University of Florida before being drafted in the first round by the Houston Oilers. Rod Smart, better known as "He Hate Me," began his professional career with the Xtreme Football League (XFL). Since the (XFL) permitted players to print words other than their last names on the back of their jerseys, possibly the most notorious jersey belonged to Lakeland Dreadnaught graduate,

Rod Smart, when he had, “He Hate Me”, imprinted on his jersey. From the XFL, Smart began his tenure in the National Football League (NFL) playing running back for the Carolina Panthers.

The Community and Facilities

DEMOGRAPHICALLY, LAKELAND IS not a particularly affluent community. Many of the athletes living in Lakeland, Florida, have parents and grandparents who grew up in the same area. The community support for the football program, however, is nothing short of awesome. The facilities that Lakeland possesses are quite respectable, and give players a sense of being part of something extraordinary. The football stadium has a capacity of ten thousand, including seating in both end zones, which adds to the excitement of Friday nights. The locker room is spacious with pictures throughout the facility reflecting big wins over the years. The team meeting room is comparable to many smaller college programs. Throughout the locker room, weight room, and team meeting room, one cannot miss the sense of tradition and history of Dreadnaught football. The pictures filling the rooms add a personal touch and inspire current athletes as they look back at the achievements of those who have gone before them.

Aside from the coaching staff and the strength program, community support is also a large factor contributing to the success of Lakeland football. Community support for Lakeland football is evidenced through the football booster club. The booster club took out a loan for four hundred thousand dollars to purchase the end zone scoreboard that shows instant replays throughout the game. Currently, the booster club solicits community members and alumni for funds to help pay off the loan on the scoreboard. The booster club collects money for the football program in two major ways. First, the money for the booster club membership dues goes straight to the program. Second, a golf tournament is held annually as a fundraiser. Like most booster clubs, members have the option of paying varying amounts of money to receive varying levels of membership. The booster club is very proactive when extra expenses are incurred. One example of this would be the purchasing of rings for the players after a state championship.

Spring Football in Florida

IN THE STATE of Florida, schools are permitted to hold twenty days of spring football. The first three days are without pads. Then, the players are allowed to practice in full gear for the remainder of the spring. Teams in Florida are also allowed to participate in one spring game or scrimmage as part of the twenty days. The Lakeland Dreadnaughts elect to participate in a full game at the conclusion of their spring. The duration of spring football in Florida, including the opportunity to play a full game, gives coaches the opportunity to evaluate talent prior to fall practice. This amount of time permitted for practice in the spring also proves advantageous when playing out-of-state teams whose states don't lend them the same opportunities for practice prior to the fall.

Miami Northwestern High School

Miami, Florida

Overview

IF THERE IS one American high school that stands above all others in its ability to produce NFL players, it is Miami Northwestern. Founded in 1951, Miami Northwestern football provides many student athletes opportunities to better lives. This football program has produced state championships in 1995, 1998, 2006, and 2007. The Miami Northwestern Bulls wrapped up the last two Florida 6A state titles in an undefeated fashion going 30-0 over the past two seasons. According to the *USA Today* national polls, Miami Northwestern has finished in the top five three times in the last ten years, including a number one national ranking in 2007.

The school itself is located across the street from a poor housing project. Miami Northwestern football proves that affluent

affluent communities aren't the only places where dynasties exist. The school itself shares Traz Powell Stadium, an off-campus stadium, with nine other schools. They must schedule games from Wednesdays through Saturdays to accommodate all of the schools sharing the stadium. Head Coach Billy Rolle estimates that around eighty-five percent of his players' parents attended Miami Northwestern. Utilizing a no-huddle spread offense, the team is electrifying to watch. Though the football program has had its share of controversy in the past, the new staff has worked diligently to restore the image of both the football program and school.

The Headlines

IN THE FALL of 2006, Miami Northwestern running back Antwain Easterling had a lot going in his favor. He was rated one of the best running backs in the nation, and was being recruited by: the University of Miami, the University of Florida, and the University of Notre Dame, among other elite collegiate programs. The Miami Northwestern Bulls were on their way to their first state football championship since 1998. Easterling had rushed for 2,831 yards and 33 touchdowns during the 2006 season. On December 7, 2006, things changed for eighteen year-old Easterling when he was arrested and charged with lewd and lascivious battery of a minor for having consensual sex with a fourteen year-old girl on the campus of Miami Northwestern High School. Two others were charged as well. Antwain Easterling was allowed to play in the 2006 state championship game two days after his arrest; he scored a touchdown and rushed for 157 yards claiming a victory for the Bulls.

An investigation following the incident revealed that a cover-up was involved in this incident. Some employees in the school district had been notified about the incident without taking the information to the proper authorities. At the conclusion of this investigation by Miami Dade School's Superintendent Rudy Crew, the outcome resulted in the firing of twenty-one people. Included in the firing were: Principal Dwight Bernard, Head Football Coach Roland Smith, and additional coaches. Miami Northwestern Athletic Director Gregory resigned as well.

In June of 2007, Principal Bernard was indicted by a Miami-Dade grand jury for failing to report the incident to authorities. Unfortunately, the hard work of many innocent players was tarnished by this incident; the accomplishments of the team and individuals were marred by the scandal.

Antwain Easterling was permitted to enroll in a pretrial diversionary program, thus allowing him to avoid prosecution and have the charges dropped. The stipulation of this was completing twenty-six weeks of counseling. Although the major colleges backed away from their interest in Easterling, he was granted a second chance. The University of Southern Mississippi signed him on a scholarship—he plays for them today.

The Rebirth

WITH THE 2007 season fast approaching, and a contest with Carroll High School from Southlake, Texas just around the corner, Miami Northwestern needed a coach. The Bulls chose to stabilize the football program by hiring someone to drive it in a different direction, turning to its former head coach, Billy Rolle. Rolle had filled the position of head coach at Miami Northwestern during the late 1990's, ultimately leaving the program after the 2000 season. In 1998, Rolle coached Miami Northwestern to a state championship and a number four national ranking, according to *USA Today*. Lowndes High School coach Randy McPherson called the 1998 Miami Northwestern team the best team he has ever seen.

Head Coach Billy Rolle understood that taking over the 2007 program was a much bigger challenge than when he took charge of the program the first time through. As a late summer hire, Rolle not only had to quickly prepare the team to play the hire, Rolle not only had to quickly prepare the team to play the upcoming season, but more importantly, focus his attention on cleaning up the school's tarnished image. Working alongside Miami Northwestern's new principal, Charles Hankerson (the fourth principal in two years), Rolle set out to rebuild the school's reputation.

With both new men on the job, positive changes began to transpire at Miami Northwestern. First, overall school attendance drastically improved. Next, Rolle instituted a mandatory after school study table on Tuesdays and Thursdays for his athletes; all players attend this prior to practice. Additionally, the football team reports to school from 9:00-Noon on Saturday mornings for a study table following Friday night games. Lastly, they implemented a dress code, which included polo shirts with the school's insignia, being worn by all students. Hankerson and Rolle are clearly vigilant at reestablishing a positive image for the school.

The Big Game

WHEN BILLY ROLLE returned to Miami Northwestern, he had both the opportunity and the challenge of a lifetime ahead of him. His team was set to travel out-of-state for the first time ever to take on perennial Texas powerhouse, Carroll High School, at Southern Methodist University in Dallas; this game generated many storylines. In terms of titles, the game featured the defending Texas 5A state champion against the defending Florida 6A state champion. Since these two states are often compared to each other, people debate which of the two states produces the best high school football programs. Carroll came into the game carrying an 80-1 record after moving up to the highest classification in Texas. Carroll was also riding a forty-nine game winning streak, tying them for the longest winning streak for a large classification school in Texas. If they beat Miami Northwestern, they would move their streak to fifty and own the record themselves.

This game also marked the third time in twenty-five years when the top two teams in the USA Today Prep Poll would meet; it was the first time that the top two teams were out-of-state opponents. Paragon Marketing, the group that would organize the game, referred to this game as the highest profile high school game ever.

This game between Miami Northwestern and Carroll carried notable distinctions between socioeconomic, racial, and facility differences of the two schools. Carroll is from a privileged area containing neighborhoods with million dollar homes. In contrast, Miami Northwestern is situated in close proximity to underprivileged housing projects. Carroll is a predominantly Caucasian school with over ninety percent of its students reported as white. In contrast, Miami Northwestern is a predominantly African-American school with over ninety percent of its students reported as black. Carroll possesses its own fifteen million dollar stadium, contains a state of the art weight room, and has an indoor practice field. In contrast, Miami Northwestern shares an off-campus stadium with nine other teams, owns a mediocre weight room, and has two grass practice fields for the whole program. The above differences were three of the many story lines that people talked about as the game approached.

The game itself would be watched on ESPNU by spectators across the country; it drew 31,896 fans and lived up to its billing. The Miami Herald reported that over four thousand Miami Northwestern faithful followed their team to Dallas to see the game. The Bulls' marching band also made the trip after collecting twenty-one thousand dollars to fund their travels. In the end, Miami Northwestern's speed was too much for Carroll to handle and the Bulls departed Dallas with a 29-21 victory. This win would solidify the first National Championship for the school if they would be able to run the table and win their second consecutive state championship.

The 2007 Team

RIDING THE MOMENTUM of the monumental performance in Dallas against Carroll, the Miami Northwestern Bulls extended their winning streak to twenty-nine games heading into the state championship game against undefeated Boone. Boone High School was not only undefeated, but had an advantage over Miami Northwestern because the state finals would be played in Orlando, a location close to their home. Miami Northwestern hoped for their second straight state championship and their first national championship—both just one win away. In the end, Miami Northwestern beat Boone 41-0 in convincing fashion. The Bulls' quarterback, Jacory Harris, recorded his forty-ninth touchdown of the season during this game; it was the second highest in Florida history. Throughout the season, Miami Northwestern outscored their opponents by a margin of 628-134—not bad for a coaching staff that was remodeled only weeks before the season's start.

The 2007 team will go down as one of the best in high school football history. Eight players from that team went on to sign scholarships with the University of Miami, four of whom would graduate from high school a semester early and enroll at the University of Miami at the beginning of 2008. In addition to the eight Miami signees, three other players signed scholarships at Division One schools. This was the largest recruiting class at Miami Northwestern since the 1998 team that sent nineteen players to sign scholarships at Division Two schools or higher, seven of whom signed Division One scholarships. Head Coach Rolle projects nine more players signing some level of scholarships from the 2007 team after they qualify academically. Coach Rolle believes that six of the eleven players who signed Division One scholarships from the 2007 team have legitimate chances of playing in the NFL if they stay healthy.

The NFL

MIAMI NORTHWESTERN HIGH School has more players in the NFL than any of the other eleven schools portrayed in this writing. They possibly have more in the NFL than any high school in the entire country. Some of the Miami Northwestern players who have made it to the NFL include: Vernon Morency (running back, Green Bay Packers), Vernon Carey (offensive tackle, Miami Dolphins), Melvin Bratton (running back, Miami Dolphins), Torrie Cox (cornerback, Tampa Bay Buccaneers), Brett Perriman (Detroit Lions, Miami Dolphins), Nate Wesster (linebacker, Denver Broncos), and Tony Martin (San Diego Chargers, Atlanta Falcons, Miami Dolphins). Marvin "Snoop" Minnis, Magic Benton, and Antonio Bryant are also NFL wide receivers. Former Miami Northwestern standout Marvin Jones, a retired NFL linebacker, was one of the most heralded linebackers to come out of Florida State University. Tolbert Bain and Khalil Jones are also two big-time players at the University of Miami from Miami Northwestern High School.

The Academics

IN 2003, A documentary about Miami Northwestern was released. The player featured in the documentary was Taurean Charles. Charles went on to sign a scholarship to the University of Florida, but is yet to see the field. The documentary highlighted the difficulty that some face in the inner city when trying to qualify academically for an athletic scholarship. While this is somewhat true, the four players from the 2007 team show that it is possible for players to graduate a semester ahead of their classes and enroll in college early as well.

The Program

MIAMI NORTHWESTERN HIGH School is on a rotating, four-period day. This means that students take eight classes per semester, but rotate between four classes one day and four different classes the next. During the football season, the offense is in a class together and the defense is in a class together on different days. The team lifts two days per week during the class, and reviews film or implements their game plan on other days. Coach Rolle is the only coach in the class with either the entire offense or entire defense.

In the off-season, the team follows the Bigger, Faster, Stronger weight lifting program. On average, around sixty players participate in workouts each day after school. Another one of the secrets to the development of the players and team is how physical the practices are at Miami Northwestern. In a day and age when many teams rarely go best offense on best defense during practice, the Bulls take the opposite approach. Not only does Miami Northwestern have the best offense practice against the best defense, but they do this live. The coaches feel they have enough depth that they are not as worried about losing players to injuries as other coaches are. This approach is even taken on Mondays and Tuesdays throughout the season. The coaching staff believes that this no holds barred mentality leads to greater success on Friday nights. Judging by the results in 2007, it is hard for one to disagree.

PART II

Chapter 14

The Systems

2007 Offenses

2007 Stats	Rush	Pass	Total	Pts/Game	Pts Allowed/Game
Carroll (Southlake)	217	301	518	44.5	19.5
Central Catholic	238	123	361	38.3	10.5
Colerain	305	80	385	37.3	9.8
De La Salle	248	150	398	46.8	11.5
Evangel	268	105	373	34.3	14.2
Independence	254	145	399	37.2	15.3
Jenks	237	201	438	45.4	13
Katy	237	154	391	43.8	8.3
Lakeland	250	84	334	28.6	15.9
Lowndes	267	41	308	29.9	7.9
Miami Northwestern	153	237	390	41.9	9.5
South Panola	294	74	368	33.3	14.3
Average	247	141	388	38.4	12.5

Statistics taken from Maxpreps.com

When looking at the 2007 offensive statistics for each of the twelve teams, one thing quickly stands out as common amongst each offense—each team runs the football effectively. While only three of the twelve programs threw the football for more than two hundred yards a game, eleven of the twelve programs rushed for at least two hundred yards a game. While the style of offense varies from program to program, all of these teams generate plenty of offense through running the football. Interestingly the four teams that ran a version of the spread offense in 2007, De La Salle, Evangel, Miami Northwestern, and Carroll, were all very good at generating offense through the ground as well.

De La Salle High School ran the Houston Split Back Veer for the first twenty-eight years of Head Coach Bob Ladouceur's tenure, but switched to a spread offense in 2007. De La Salle implemented this change to actually make it easier to run the football. With the team finding it more difficult to run the football against eight or nine man fronts, they altered their offense. De La Salle still averaged close to two hundred-fifty yards a game on the ground in 2007 while still utilizing option principles, but they did it out of spread formations.

Carroll High School plays with either four or five receivers on the field at a time throughout the course of a game, and relies on the quarterback to generate much of the team's rushing offense. Miami Northwestern depends on their quarterback to help out in the running game as well. Carroll and Miami Northwestern are the only two teams out of the twelve that operate without a huddle for the entire game. Jenks and Carroll were the only two of the twelve schools that rushed and passed for over two hundred yards a game.

Another byproduct of the offensive system a team uses is somewhat connected to the points each of these teams allows per game. Carroll High School, for example, passed the football more than any of the twelve schools. Carroll also gave up more points per game than the rest of the schools. One of the things that is often overlooked is that teams that throw the football often, increase the number of offensive and defensive series throughout a game, thus making the games longer. As a result, the number of possessions that the Carroll Dragons have to defend throughout the course of a game is much higher than schools such as Colerain and Lowndes who rely heavily on strong rushing attacks on offense. With Carroll averaging three hundred-one yards passing each game, compared to Lowndes and Colerain at forty and eighty-one yards respectively, the three schools have big differences in the number of opposing team possessions to defend over the course of game and a season. While Lowndes gave up an average of 7.9 points per game and Colerain gave up 9.8 points per game, Carroll gave up the most points per game out of any of the schools at 19.5 points per game. While any team that allows less than ten points per game as an average is considered to have a dominant defense, teams that depend on throwing the football will find it much harder to have a defense giving up less than ten points per game.

With the twelve programs averaging over thirty-eight points per game amongst them in 2007, it is interesting to notice how many different types of offenses were used among the programs. De La Salle, Evangel, Miami Northwestern, and Carroll all run a variation of the spread offense. Lowndes runs the Wing T offense. Colerain uses multiple formations to run the triple option, as a foundation to their offense. Colerain's head coach, Tom Bolden, feels that his offensive system allows his teams to compete against much larger high schools that they normally might not be successful against if they ran a traditional offense. Central Catholic, Jenks, Katy, and Lakeland run multiple sets on offense. All four of these schools rely heavily on traditional two back formations as well as other sets. Lastly, Independence and South Panola run primarily one back formations. While the type of systems that each of the programs use varies, the common denominator is that they all run the ball well.

Tracking the Last Four Years

Points Scored	2007	2006	2005	2004	Avg.
Carroll (Southlake)	44.5	44.3	47.8	45	45.4
Central Catholic	38.3	28.8	27	33.8	32.5
Colerain	37.3	33.9	43.6	46.3	40.3
De La Salle	46.8	41.7	37.9	31.8	39.6
Evangel	34.3	37.3	36.5	37.2	36.4
Independence	37.2	41.5	38.5	56.2	43.6
Jenks	45.4	35.9	32.1	39	38.4
Katy	43.8	33.2	38.1	31.7	37
Lakeland	28.6	39.1	38.7	40.2	35.2
Lowndes	29.9	20.1	36	37.3	31.8
Miami Northwestern	41.9	43.3	24.9	20.7	34.1
South Panola	33.3	30.4	38.4	37.9	35.1
Average	38.4	35.8	36.6	38.1	37.5

Points Allowed	2007	2006	2005	2004	Avg.
Carroll (Southlake)	19.5	11.2	16	20.1	16.6
Central Catholic	10.5	10.4	9.8	9.6	10.1
Colerain	9.8	6.4	9.6	6.5	8
De La Salle	11.5	15.2	12.3	13.8	13.3
Evangel	14.2	11.1	13.4	18.6	14.3
Independence	15.3	15.4	13.9	8.8	13.3
Jenks	13	12.7	20.6	13.9	14.8
Katy	8.3	8.1	12.2	13.3	10.4
Lakeland	15.9	11.5	6.2	11.9	10.6
Lowndes	7.9	13.9	6.7	6.7	8.3
Miami Northwestern	9.5	7.2	10.8	17.1	10.7
South Panola	14.3	9.4	10.1	10	11
Average	12.5	11	11.8	12.5	11.8

Statistics taken from Maxpreps.com

nr=Not ranked in the top 25 that year

USA Today Rankings	1998	1999	2000	2001	2002	2003	2004	2005	2006	2007	Total Top 25
De La Salle; Concord, CA	1	3	1	1	1	1	nr	23	14	3	9
Independence; Charlotte, NC	nr	nr	nr	6	3	4	2	3	8	nr	6
Jenks; Jenks, OK	nr	15	3	2	nr	nr	21	nr	18	18	6
Carroll; Southlake, TX	nr	nr	nr	nr	12	19	1	2	1	nr	5
South Panola; Batesville, MS	nr	nr	nr	nr	nr	9	7	6	9	9	5
Northwestern; Miami, FL	4	nr	nr	nr	nr	25	nr	nr	5	1	4
Lakeland; Lakeland, FL	nr	6	nr	nr	nr	nr	18	1	3	nr	4
Evangel Christian; Shreveport, LA	3	2	nr	12	19	nr	nr	nr	nr	nr	4
Katy; Katy, TX	nr	nr	6	nr	nr	18		nr	nr	4	3
Colerain; Cincinnati, OH	nr	nr	nr	nr	nr	nr	5	nr	23	14	3
Central Catholic; Pittsburgh, PA	nr	nr	nr	nr	nr	nr	6	nr	nr	11	2
Lowndes; Valdosta, GA	nr	nr	nr	nr	nr	nr	11	11	nr	nr	2

nr=Not ranked in the top 25 that year

Throughout the past ten years, no team has dominated high school football like De La Salle High School. From 1998 to 2007, De La Salle claimed five of the ten national championships according to *USA Today*. Impressively, De La Salle has only failed to finish in the top twenty-five in the nation once during the past ten years. That year was in 2004—the same year their one hundred fifty-one game winning streak came to an end.

It is interesting to observe that in the past ten years, only once, in 1999, did the *USA Today* National Champion not come from one of these twelve phenomenal programs. De La Salle (5), Carroll (2), Lakeland (1), Miami Northwestern (1) are the four schools that have *USA Today* National Championships to their names in the past ten years. Overall, these twelve programs have clearly dominated high school football not only in their own states, but also at the national level.

When studying the defenses over the past four years, Colerain and Lowndes stand out in that they averaged 8.0 and 8.3 points allowed a game, respectively. These two programs were the only two of the twelve that held opponents to fewer than ten points per game for the four year period. Both Lowndes and Colerain actually each held opponents to less than seven points per game two of the past four seasons. By studying the 2007 offensive numbers, these two teams relied more on running the football than any of the other programs. Colerain and Lowndes passed the football for the fewest number of yards per game in 2007. This seems to suggest that each of these programs relies on a ground game that allows them to control the clock and force opponents to score with a limited number of possessions throughout a game. Both programs deserve to be very proud of the caliber of defense they have established.

The single best defensive effort during the last four years can be argued to have come from one of two places in the state of Florida. If one looks at the just the pure numbers, it will be found that the 2005 Lakeland team went on to finish first in the nation, according to *USA Today*, while allowing a meager average of 6.2 points per game over the course of the season. However, the Miami Northwestern defenses of 2006 and 2007 might have been even better. While the Miami Northwestern teams in 2006 allowed 7.2 and 9.5 points per game respectively, the Bulls' squad relied heavily on throwing the football when they were on offense. As a result, the Bulls' defense was on the field for more possessions throughout the course of both seasons. To put the Miami Northwestern's impressive numbers in perspective, one only needs to look at Carroll's numbers as they also were a team that relied on throwing the football. Carroll gave up an average of 16.6 points per game over the past four seasons. And so, the school that had the best defense for one year would probably be located somewhere in the state of Florida.

As for the offenses during the past four years, only Carroll, Colerain, and Independence have averaged over forty points per game. Carroll's no huddle spread offense led all teams with a 45.4 point average scored per game over the past four years. Colerain was the only program to finish in the top three regarding points scored *and* the top three in points allowed. The, 2004 Independence Patriots could easily be argued as having the single best offense in the past four years. The 2004 Patriots not only averaged 56.2 points per game on offense, but allowed only 8.8 points per game on defense throughout the course of the seventeen-game season. In 2004, Independence played seven games in which they scored over sixty points, one game they won 75-0, and one more they won 85-9.

Chapter 15

Common Denominators

Thriving Strength Programs

PROBABLY THE EASIEST common denominator to recognize amongst the twelve programs is the priority that is placed on the strength programs. While the specific programs vary, each program benefits greatly from having a thriving strength program. Interestingly, each head coach speaks to the *non-physical* benefits of a highly structured and demanding strength program, as well as the physical benefits.

De La Salle's Head Coach Bob Ladouceur views the off-season strength program as the number one way to bring his squad into a tightly bonded team. Lakeland's Head Coach Bill Castle admits that there is a strong correlation between the overall physical strength of his teams and the successes they have achieved in any given year. Independence's Head Coach Tom Knotts believes that two key outcomes to the team's off-season program are that the players develop self-confidence and strong work ethics. Colerain's Head Coach Tom Bolden believes the strength and conditioning program is extremely important for his school in order to compensate for not having spring football as many other states do. Any way it's viewed, all twelve of these head coaches place high priorities on the off-season programs and consider them to be foundational to their successes.

When studying the specific programs that each school uses, it is clear that there are a variety of programs and beliefs amongst the schools. Five of the twelve schools (Colerain, De La Salle, Jenks, Lakeland, and South Panola) all, for the most part, are on a four day per week split workout schedule. Two days per week their players are focusing on upper body lifts; two days per week, on lower body lifts. Three of the programs (Miami Northwestern, Lowndes, and Evangel) follow the Bigger, Faster, Stronger program. While Miami Northwestern and Lowndes follow this program very closely, Evangel uses only a portion of it and combines some of the Louisiana State University (LSU) program that their defensive coordinator went through while playing at LSU. The players in the Central Catholic program lift three days per week. They utilize a program that was developed and run by current NFL strength coaches; these coaches created Central Catholic's program prior to going to the NFL. Independence and Katy athletes follow a five day per week lifting program. Lastly, Carroll players lift three days per week one week, and two days a week the next.

While the majority of these programs do the bulk of off-season training during a school day athletic period, Colerain High School trains after school to establish a better coach to player ratio. While it is possible to have one coach with a class of thirty or forty players, the workout is more efficiently run if the ratio of coach to player is better. Programs that have only one coach running a weightlifting class often conduct the entire workout on command with a whistle. Lakeland High School, for example, has three classes of thirty athletes in a weight room with ten multipurpose workstations. One coach runs the entire workout with a whistle signaling to each group when the set is to begin. While the workouts at Lakeland are very organized and fast paced, it doesn't seem the ideal situation especially when some schools are able to have their entire coaching staff present during the school day workouts. Having the entire coaching staff present at each off-season workout is the ideal situation but not a prerequisite for having a quality strength program.

Some of the schools have a bonus to their strength program. A few of the programs that have middle schools fully feeding into the high school have the seventh and eighth graders participating in the same strength program as the high school. An example of this is Lowndes High School in Valdosta, Georgia. The middle school coaching staff puts the seventh and eighth graders through the Bigger, Faster, Stronger Program just like the high school players. This not only benefits the middle school kids from a physical standpoint, but it also gives the middle school players familiarity with the high school strength program system prior to arriving at the high school.

For the most part, each of the twelve programs emphasizes many of the same core lifts. The top four lifts emphasized are: the back squat, dead lift, bench press, and some variation of the power clean; some of these programs have their players perform hang cleans instead of power cleans. De La Salle High School is the only program of the twelve that also emphasizes the snatch as a core lift.

While there are differences between the schools regarding the type of lifting program that each school implements as a support structure, a thriving strength program is a consistency amongst these schools. These strength programs create more depth on the teams, thus allowing for fewer players to play both offense and defense. Injuries also do not seem to have as big of an impact on these programs when compared to others because of the overall depth of these teams. Lastly, the vital non-physical benefits resulting from these strength programs are often overlooked. During the off-seasons, these athletes unite together to forge bonds based on the rigorous workouts they endure—this results in an undeniable team unity.

To Play Both Ways?

WITH THE VERY large numbers of players participating in these programs, and thriving strength and conditioning programs being the greatest common denominator amongst them, the way they are structured is important. Eleven of the twelve programs have their coaches specialize in either offense or defense. Ten of the twelve programs have their players play either offense or defense. Lowndes is the only program that has their athletes practice both sides of the football while coaches specialize in either offense or defense. De La Salle High School is the sole program where the coaches will coach both offense and defense and the players will practice both as well.

There are four main benefits to structuring a program in such a way where the coaches specialize in either offense or defensive with the players doing the same. The first benefit is that coaches can spend all of their time specializing on one side of the ball. When a coach goes to a clinic or is trying to improve as a coach, he can devote all of his time to refining the position he coaches, which in turn will better the overall ability of the coaching staff. During the season, the coaches also will have the advantage of spending all of their time preparing for the opposing teams' offenses or defenses. A coach can become more prepared for what he will see on Friday night if all of his time has been focused on either his opponent's offense or defense.

The second benefit to this way of structuring a program is that each player has the opportunity to become very skilled at the one position he plays. This not only aids the players in being able to execute their given assignments, but it also fosters greater competition at practices. Coaches now have the option of practicing the starting defense against the starting offense as often as they choose.

The third benefit of this structure has to do with the stamina of a football team on two levels. During the course of a football game, if one team has many players playing both offense and defense while the opposing team has a separate offense and defense, the first team better have some sort of lead going into the fourth quarter because of the fact that their opponent should be fresher at the end the game. On the second level, with athletes playing fewer plays throughout the season, that team will be fresher physically by the end of the season when teams are preparing for playoff runs. Some teams with athletes playing both sides of the ball wear down towards the end of the season and are not able to put forth their best effort when it really counts. An example of this was seen in Jenks High School of Oklahoma. Jenks had been a program where the athletes played both offense and defense. After a few key late-season losses, the coaching staff at Jenks felt that their teams were worn down at the end of the year and not playing their best—so they changed their philosophy.

The last benefit to having players play either offense or defense is that a team can put fresher and more talented players on special teams. Special teams, an often-overlooked component of a football game, is a component that often determines the outcome of a game. Teams that have players playing offense and defense are faced with the decision of either inserting tired players on the field for special teams, or putting less talented, but fresh players, on the field.

After studying these twelve programs, it is clear that this type of system is a huge factor to their success. While some regions in the country find this as the norm, many programs either don't structure themselves this way, or do not have the depth of developed talent to make this transition successfully. One significant reason these programs can structure themselves like this with a successful outcome is not as much related to the overall numbers of players in their programs, but more related to their strength and conditioning programs. The thriving strength and conditioning programs develop players from the time they enter the program until the time they leave. As a result, more athletes are capable of playing football at high levels in these programs when compared against other programs.

Teams that separate their players between offense and defense tend to put their better players on defense. Lowndes' Head Coach, Randy McPherson, agrees with this statement but adds that coaches don't always put their best players on defense fully; Lowndes does try to put their best players on defense—period. McPherson's program is not like the majority of the other programs studied, for it is only Lowndes and De La Salle that will split practice time in half, devoting time equally to offense and defense. McPherson has the defensive players back up the starting offense because when Lowndes offense is struggling to move the ball throughout the course of a game, they then can put their better players on the field to help the offense move the ball and score. McPherson believes that coaches who say they put their best players on defense really don't because they would have a tough time scoring if they did. McPherson believes Lowndes would have a tough time scoring consistently if they didn't have their best players, who play primarily defense, play offense as well at times.

De La Salle High School is run very similarly to Lowndes in this aspect. De La Salle's Head Coach Bob Ladouceur chooses to split practice time between offense and defense with his coaches splitting time between them as well. Ladouceur believes he has enough talent to put a separate offense and defense on the field, but when players get injured, the talent of the backups drops off too much if he doesn't have the defensive starters supporting offensive positions; the offensive starters can back up the defensive players as well. As a result, at De La Salle one would expect to see additional two-way players in games as the season stretched on and injuries accumulated.

While the other ten programs sometimes have a few players, at most, playing both offense and defense, the coaching staffs and players work on offense *or* defense for the entirety of the practice. They do not do both. The few exceptional players, who are too good to not be used on both sides of the ball, will then split their time between offense and defense at practice while the rest of their teammates and coaches focus their time on only one side. In summary each of the twelve programs try to have as few players as possible playing both offense and defense. Eleven of the twelve coaching staffs coach only one side of the football. These programs have enough developed talent to make this a successful formula because of their thriving strength and conditioning program.

Consistency of Systems

A THIRD COMMON denominator amongst the twelve schools is the fact that they change very little from year to year. These programs tweak their offense or defense from year to year to utilize their talent more efficiently; it is extremely rare, however, to see dramatic overhauls of their systems. If one of these coaches has a quarterback in his system that is exceptional, the team might put the ball in the air with that quarterback more than they would if he weren't there. The coaches may add a few more routes. Nevertheless, you won't see these coaches going from the I formation to a spread offense from year to year.

One exception to this is De La Salle High School (California). For the first twenty-eight years of Bob Ladouceur's tenure at De La Salle, the offense could best be described as a Houston Split Back Veer team. After the 2006 season, Ladouceur found it tougher and tougher to run the football efficiently as teams would put eight and nine players close to the line of scrimmage in attempts to stop De La Salle's running game. Resulting from this, Ladouceur, who strongly believes that at the high school level teams must be able to run the football efficiently regardless of what the defenses try to do, decided to change things up a bit. In 2007, De La Salle came out in a new look where they still ran option principles, but out of multiple spread formations in order to spread defenses out helping De La Salle run the football more effectively.

Surprisingly, only six of the twelve head coaches have control over the middle schools feeding directly into them. Out of the nine public schools studied, four of them don't have middle schools as direct feeds, but rather gain their students from a variety of schools. While it varies as to when the players start running the high school systems, or some variation of it, all of them engrain their systems into their players as soon as they can and seldom deviate from it.

What is very consistent amongst these programs is that they don't switch their systems from year to year depending on the type of athletes they have. These coaches believe they benefit more from having players enter the varsity program with the base offense and defense already down than they would if they started from scratch each year with a new system tailored to the current team. Another benefit of this consistency is that coaching staffs get more precise at generating answers for the different ways teams try to attack their systems. The more experience a staff has within a system, the better they become at coaching it.

Team Building

A MAJOR COMMON denominator amongst these programs is their huge emphasis on team building. Although each of the programs uses varying methods for bringing individuals into a closely knit group, to all of the programs, it is a priority. Jenks' (Oklahoma) Head Coach Allan Trimble said it best when he stated that if a program doesn't place team building as the highest priority, they are going to be in trouble.

De La Salle's (California) commitment card program is unique. Beginning in 1992, the Spartans of De la Salle have been faithful in this weekly team building exercise for the last sixteen years. The Carroll Dragons (Texas) mold their players into one united group through the Dragon Maker portion of their off-season program coupled with their six hour team meeting prior to the season's start. Jenks' (Oklahoma) players participate in a summer retreat where they partake in a wide range of team building activities. Lowndes' (Georgia) varsity program finds tremendous unity in the time they spend together at a Fellowship of Christian Athletes Camp. When asked about team building and Katy (Texas) football, Head Coach Gary Joseph spoke first about his players' common faith in God. The three private schools (Central Catholic, De La Salle, and Evangel) all share a unity within their programs based around a common faith in God. Independence (North Carolina) Head Coach Tom Knotts feels that he brushed off team building in 2007, and his team paid for it. Knotts also made it very clear that team building will be a major emphasis in his program from 2008 forth.

In meeting with all twelve of these head coaches, it was clear that the rigorous off-season strength and conditioning programs are huge team builders. De La Salle Head Coach Bob Ladouceur made the point that the off-season program was his team's number one team builder. Jenks deliberately holds their summer pride workouts at 6:00 AM for the very purpose of making their players commit in order to be part of the program. It is clear from all twelve of the programs that their athletes form strong bonds from their shared experiences of going through the demanding off-season programs together.

No matter what methods or means a program uses to transform a group of individuals into a tightly united team, these programs have shown it must be a priority. Talented players are regularly defeated by united teams that share a common purpose and commitment to each other. An emphasis on team building is a clear common denominator amongst all twelve of these gridiron dynasties.

Chapter 16

Program Comparisons

How Much Talent?

WHILE SOME HIGH school programs will go many years without a signing class of more than two Division One players, eight out of the twelve programs in this book have had at least five Division One players signed in at least one of the last five years. On the other hand, one would naturally expect that these programs would all be pumping out at least three Division One players per year, but this is not true. Actually, only four of the twelve programs have averaged three or more Division One players each season spanning the past seven years.

What is important to note is that these programs are consistently successful year in and year out with or without great individual talent. De La Salle High School (California) has averaged less than two Division One players each season while still winning three national titles and one third place finish over the past seven years—this is according to *USA Today*. For the most part, these programs are competing for state championships each year. When they gain a wave of very good talent, they are competing for national championships.

The following list was taken from http://www.scout.com. The numbers of Division One players are likely close, but a little low if anything. Sometimes, players who sign after the initial signing date because of being late academic qualifiers, or for other reasons, are not listed on this website. The chart does, however, lend an idea of how much Division One talent has been pulled from these twelve programs over the past seven years. The chart also illustrates which colleges these players are entering.

School	2007	2006	2005	2004	2003	2002	2001	Total	Where they are sending them:
Miami Northwestern	11	2	3	6	3	4	3	32	Miami (13), South Florida (3), Florida State (2)
Evangel	2	2	6	2	3	5	6	26	Louisiana Tech (4), Louisiana Monroe (4), Texas Tech (3)
Carroll (Southlake)	6	4	9	2	3	2	0	26	North Texas (4), Rice (3), Texas (2), Missouri (2)
Colerain	5	2	6	6	1	1	0	21	Cincinnati (8), Ohio State (4), Michigan (3)
South Panola	4	4	1	3	3	2	1	18	Mississippi (7), Southern Mississippi (4)
Jenks	3	4	1	3	0	1	4	16	Tulsa (3), Oklahoma (2), Air Force (2),
Lakeland	1	10	3	1	1	0	0	16	Florida (7), Florida State (1), LSU (1), Alabama (!)
Independence	2	3	2	3	0	2	2	14	Georgia (4), South Carolina (2), East Carolina (2)
De La Salle	0	1	0	1	5	3	3	13	Oregon (4), Michigan (1), Notre Dame (1), UCLA (1)

Katy	7	1	1	1	2	0	0	12	Texas A&M (2), Rice (2)
Central Catholic	5	0	0	2	0	0	2	9	Pittsburgh (4), Wisconsin (1), Syracuse (!)
Lowndes	2	0	0	3	0	0	0	5	Southern Mississippi (3), Western Michigan (1)

Statistics according to http://www.scout.com

Athletic Periods

FIVE OF THE twelve programs have the opportunity to not only train their players each day in the weight room, but also practically hold practices year round without pads. Katy (Texas), Carroll (Texas), Jenks (Oklahoma), Evangel (Louisiana), and South Panola (Mississippi) all have athletic periods in season and out of season where they can lift, run, or go outside and practice. The amount of time the coaches at these schools have to work with their players is advantageous when compared against programs without this opportunity. With this surplus of time, players can master bigger playbooks and become much more difficult to compete against. During these athletic periods, each of these programs has the chance to have every single coach in the class working with the athletes. Each assistant coach teaches both of the athletic periods as part of their teaching schedule.

One of the secrets to Katy's (Texas) success is that they do the majority of their lifting after school, thus allowing the Katy football team to practice during the majority of the athletic period time. While some programs in Texas use their athletic periods to lift and run the players without requiring after school commitments as well, Katy usually practices during their athletic periods and then lift and run after school.

Eight of the nine public schools studied in this book train their players during the day in some form. Miami Northwestern (Florida) is the only school out of the eight that does not do it both semesters. Rather, Miami Northwestern trains their players in the weight room after school during second semester. Colerain (Ohio) is the only public school program not training their players during the day first *or* second semester. The philosophy behind this comes in the form of wanting to have all of their coaches present for the workouts. Since Colerain doesn't have an athletic period, they choose to train their team after school.

South Panola (Mississippi) leads the way with three athletic periods during a seven period day. All ten of their coaches teach these three athletic periods and four other classes, except the head coach who is the athletic coordinator, but is present for all three athletic periods as well. South Panola trains their freshmen during one period and trains their varsity players during two periods. Out of all the schools studied, South Panola has the most time with their players during the school day.

Out of the three private schools, Evangel (Louisiana), Central Catholic (Pennsylvania) and De La Salle (California), Evangel is the only one that trains their players during the school day. Evangel begins each school day with their athletic period.

One of the major benefits for all of the programs that train their players during the school day is that it allows for athletes to participate in multiple sports and lift weights year round without football practice interfering. If those schools did not have the opportunity to train players during the day, players would be faced with the decision of training or playing another sport. If schools can train players during the day, athletes are not put in the position of having to choose.

Youth Football

WHILE IT WAS expected that large numbers of these programs would have elementary aged youth football teams affiliated with them, not all of them did. Only half of these twelve schools have one of these systems in place. Evangel Christian Academy, in Shreveport, Louisiana, just recently began a youth football program even though Evangel has demonstrated tremendous success for many years without the youth program.

It is also interesting that some of these programs do not even have middle school teams feeding directly into them. As a result, half of the programs studied don't have any control of the programs feeding into them because, as in the cases of the two Florida schools, there is simply no football at the middle school level *or* the programs simply don't have full middle schools feeding into them.

With the six schools that do have organized youth football programs, the high school coaches understand that solid people must be coaching these teams to ensure that young athletes don't have bad experiences during their first attempts at football. The high school coaches recognize that if a young player has a bad experience, he might never make it to the high school program thus eliminating the possibility of helping the high school program. Colerain High School (Ohio) is so aware of this danger that parents aren't allowed to coach the youth teams. Colerain fills the coaching spots with former players of the Colerain program and community members who don't have children playing on the youth teams.

South Panola High School (Mississippi) takes it a step further with spring football at the youth level. No matter how it's viewed, it seems the greatest benefit of having a youth football program affiliated with the high school program is the connection the players will feel at a younger age with the high school program; not the familiarity a young player will have with the high schools' schemes. While a strong youth football program can be a great benefit, what seems to be more important is what is done with the athletes once they enter high school. Youth programs certainly aren't a prerequisite for building high school football dynasties. The six programs without them provide evidence of just that.

Race and Dynasties

BY EXAMINING THESE twelve elite programs, it is apparent that high school football dynasties don't fall in one spot on the racial spectrum. The study of these twelve random schools located throughout the United States proves that a great racial diversity persists in the success of high school football. African Americans, Caucasians, Pacific Islanders, and Hispanics all comprise percentages of these top programs. Falling at different points of the ethnicity scale are two of the best teams in the nation: Florida's Miami Northwestern and Texas' Carroll High School. Miami Northwestern's football team is nearly all African American; Carroll's program is nearly all Caucasian—both of these teams demonstrate, however, that a primarily single ethnicity team can achieve success amongst mixed ethnicity teams. It seems that there is sometimes a preconceived notion that the vast majority of successful football teams are predominantly composed of one ethnicity. Remarkably, the majority of these twelve programs are fairly balanced when it comes to race. Seven of the twelve programs include at least 25% African American and 25% Caucasian on their team. It is clear to see that the myth that only one race dominates dynasties can be dispelled by the examination of these twelve outstanding programs.

Chapter 17

The Coaches

Age of the Coaches

WHEN STUDYING EACH of the programs, it is clear that the men running the programs are exceptional at what they do. All of these men could take over almost any program, given some basic community and administration support, and quickly improve the program's success. It is obvious from my time with each of these coaches that they all are very driven, well-organized, and familiar with how to win. It is also apparent that each of them is unique, thus making it nearly impossible to categorize them into types or classes.

So, how do the ages of the head coaches play a role in creating high school football dynasties? Throughout these twelve programs, two coaches are in their late 30s; they are the youngest of any of the programs. Three of the coaches are between ages 44 and 46 years old. Six of the coaches are between ages 50 and 53 years of age, and the oldest coach is 60. What seems more important are not the current ages of these coaches, but rather how old they were when they began incredible runs. In other words, how young were some of these coaches when their programs stepped up to a new level, suggesting a breaking through the learning curve stage of coaching.

Tom Knotts, the Head Coach at Independence High School in Charlotte, North Carolina, was a successful coach before coming to Independence in 2000. But, at Independence during his first year, his program exploded. The program won seven consecutive large classification state titles before losing in the state finals in 2007. In the midst of capturing state title after state title, his program won one hundred-nine consecutive games, which currently stands as the second longest winning streak in high school football history. Knotts was forty-four years old when he took over and began his impressive run at Independence.

Randy McPherson, like Knotts, held an impressive résumé when he arrived at Lowndes High School in Valdosta, Georgia. After a few building years at Lowndes, McPherson was forty-two years old when he won his first of three large classification state championships at Lowndes in a four year time span.

It took Head Coach Bill Castle ten years to win his first state championship after taking over at Lakeland. Castle was thirty-eight when Lakeland won their first title, but it was ten years later when the program exploded. When Castle was forty-eight years old, the team began a run of five state championships over a twelve year span. During this twelve year run, Lakeland also captured two national championships, one by *USA Today*.

Billy Rolle, head coach of Miami Northwestern, won his first of two state championships at Miami Northwestern when he was only thirty-five years old. The 1998 team that he coached finished the season ranked fourth in the nation according to *USA Today*. Nine years later, Rolle captured his second state championship at Miami Northwestern, this time finishing first in the *USA Today* national poll. In between the two titles, Rolle won a third as the head coach of Miami Killian High School in 2004.

Jenks High School in Jenks, Oklahoma hired a young Allan Trimble at the age of thirty-two. While some people were surely questioning whether someone so young could take Jenks to the top, those concerns and doubts were quickly put to rest. Beginning at thirty-two years of age, Trimble went on to lead Jenks to nine large classification state championships in twelve years.

Bob Ladouceur took over as the head football coach at De La Salle High School at the early age of twenty-four. Six years later, De La Salle won their first state championship. Seven years later when Ladouceur was thirty-seven years old was when De La Salle began the longest winning streak in high school football history.

From studying these twelve programs, it seems that the earliest age a head coach could expect the type of successes these programs have enjoyed is around 35 or 36. It is quite clear that there is a learning curve for any head coach. Coaches naturally improve as they acquire experience as assistant coaches; when bridging up to a head coach, the experience continues to accumulate, though at a faster rate. Once in awhile, a coach will come around who is extremely gifted, such as Allan Trimble of Jenks or Bob Ladouceur at De La Salle; they can elevate programs to dynasties at much earlier ages. One thing that is clear is that becoming a great coach, like many other things in life, comes with time.

Coaching Work Days Compared

WITH SO MUCH time invested in the role of being a head coach, examining the head coaches' work day helps to gain insight into the level of support the coaches receive from the schools they coach for. With limited hours in a day, these programs benefit from having coaches able to spend more time on football and program building. All twelve head coaches hold some sort of job on their high school campuses.

Three of the twelve head coaches are employed solely as football coaches. The head coaches at Jenks, Carroll, and Evangel all fall into this category. These coaches have the most time available to work only on football throughout both the football season and the off-season. These three coaches have ideal situations when it comes to time allotted to work on football-related activities.

Lowndes, Katy, and South Panola all have head coaches currently serving as athletic directors or athletic coordinators (different titles for the same job). The four head coaches at Colerain, Miami Northwestern, Independence, and Central Catholic hold jobs pertaining to physical education. The only one of these four head coaches that does not specifically teach weight training classes during the school day is Central Catholic Head Coach Terry Totten; he was just recently hired as the weight room supervisor.

Two of the head coaches are teachers, but do not work in the physical education department. Bill Castle of Lakeland High School serves as the schools OJT (On the Job Training) teacher. Castle, whose office is located next to the weight room with a window actually looking in, can manage students receiving credits for holding a job outside of the school. He also has some freed up time to work on football or oversee the work done in the weight room by his players while the assistant coaches run the workouts. De La Salle Head Coach Bob Ladouceur is the only one of the twelve coaches who actually teaches in the classroom. Ladouceur teaches Religious Studies at the private Catholic School in Concord, California.

These coaches have proven that coaches can hold other jobs, such as athletic director or physical education teacher, throughout the school day and still build successful programs at state and national levels. While this is true, it would be fair to deduce that the nine coaches who do not have *football only jobs* could benefit greatly from having set-ups similar to Jenks, Evangel, and Carroll where the head football coaches have the luxury of spending all of their time on building their program.

To Coordinate or Delegate

WHILE MANY DIVISION One football programs will carry around one hundred-twenty players in their program, eighty-five of whom are on football scholarships, most of the twelve high school programs studied in this book are much bigger than that. Katy High School began the 2007 season with three hundred-forty-six players in their program. Carroll High School from Southlake, Texas was even bigger with over four hundred players in their program. With programs of these sizes, the role of head coaches was something worth examining.

Out of these twelve programs, half of the head coaches do not coordinate either the offense or the defense; none of these six head coaches coach an offensive or defensive position either. These six coaches are from: Carroll, Katy, Miami Northwestern, Jenks, Colerain, and Evangel. They could best be described as overseers of their total programs and their assistant coaches. While they are very aware of the offensive and defensive game plans on a weekly basis, they do not call plays on either side of the football.

Four of the twelve head coaches serve as both offensive coordinators and head coaches. The head coaches at Lakeland, Independence, Lowndes, and De La Salle all serve in this capacity. These four coaches specialize in the offensive side of the ball, but coordinating their teams' offenses does limit how much they can oversee the defensive side of the ball. Bob Ladouceur, the Head Coach at De La Salle, has served in this dual capacity as a head coach and offensive coordinator since he began at De La Salle twenty-nine years ago. Bill Castle, the head coach at Lakeland High School, has served in this capacity at Lakeland since he began thirty-two years ago.

Two of the twelve head coaches serve as both defensive coordinators and head coaches. Head Coach Terry Totten, at Central Catholic High School, served as the team's defensive coordinator prior to being promoted to Head Coach. Totten continued to maintain his role as the defensive coordinator when he transitioned into being the head coach. For the large majority of his time as a college assistant coach, he served as a defensive coordinator. South Panola's Head Coach Lance Pogue did not coordinate either the offense or defense in 2007, but will take on the additional responsibility of coordinating the team's defense in 2008.

These twelve coaches prove that there is not one clear formula when defining their roles. While most of the head coaches do not coordinate, but rather oversee, sometimes the best thing for a program is to utilize the head coaches' expertise as seen in Terry Totten of Central Catholic. Head Coaches must examine their coaching staffs and determine whether their program will be better or worse off with them coordinating. With more years on the job, coaches learn to manage their time more efficiently, thus enabling them to take on more responsibility in the form of coordinating. When the numbers of a program get very high, as in the two examples of more than three hundred players of the two Texas programs, the head coach almost must either cut back the numbers of players, or simply choose to not coordinate but just oversee—this is out of sheer necessity.

Chapter 18

Financial Comparisons

Booster Clubs

IT MIGHT BE assumed that tremendous financial backing lies at the foundation of most of these elite programs. It is surprising that the majority of these programs actually have very average booster clubs when it comes to financial resources raised. One of the reasons this holds true is that a large amount of these schools have a booster club that includes more than just football. Colerain High School (Ohio), Independence High School (North Carolina), and Carroll High School (Texas) are three of the schools with booster clubs supporting all of their schools' sports.

The Colerain Booster Club, like many booster clubs, receives much of its funds from the membership dues paid by people wanting to be part of it. Along with membership dues oftentimes comes perks. These include parking spots for games, or the first opportunities to buy game tickets. When these funds, which often make up a bulk of the funds raised by booster clubs, are distributed amongst all of the sports, it dramatically changes the financial support of the football program. As a result, the amount of money that Colerain's football program receives in addition to the school budget ends up to be less than fifty thousand dollars. Compared with the Lowndes Booster Club (Georgia), which generates around one hundred-fifty thousand dollars annually, Colerain has one-third of what Lowndes has in financial resources. Colerain is in the process of beginning a separate booster club specifically for football.

The booster club at Carroll (Texas), which is located in the midst of a notably affluent community, gives back to the high school programs around sixty-five thousand dollars per year. Coaches at Carroll are annually asked to come up with a wish list of things they would like for their program. The booster club, which helps support the schools feeding into the high school as well, then has the task of trying to determine where they can best invest these funds. An example of this is when Carroll installed a stereo system in the school's weight room that is used by multiple sports at the school. The best fundraiser that the Carroll Booster Club takes part in is a golf tournament. The booster club, which teams up with the Parent/Teacher Organization for this fundraiser annually, splits the profits in half with the Parent/Teacher Organization. In conjunction with the golf tournament, a dinner with a live and silent auction contributes to the event as well. The total amount of money that is raised each year from this fundraiser is around one hundred thousand dollars; half of this goes toward supporting Carroll athletic teams.

While the Jenks, Lowndes, and Central Catholic programs receive high levels of financial support from their booster clubs each year, the rest of the programs prove that overwhelming financial support from a booster club isn't a common denominator among the programs studied. As Independence (North Carolina) Head Coach Tom Knotts states, "After you have everything you need for a weight room, there really isn't much else that a program truly needs." Lakeland (Florida) Head Coach Bill Castle says his booster club kicks it into high gear when they want to work on a special project like the four hundred thousand dollar scoreboard that they recently added to their stadium. While amenities such as this scoreboard are nice, by studying these programs, it seems that seems that money through booster clubs is not a prerequisite for building high school football dynasties.

Financial Disparity

WHEN COMPARING THE amount of money head coaches and assistant coaches earn at each of the schools, it is clear that there is a huge disparity amongst the programs. The range between schools in terms of how much money is put into the entire coaching staffs is immense. Jenks (Oklahoma), Katy (Texas), Carroll (Texas), and Lowndes (Georgia) seem to stand far above the rest of the programs when it comes to financial support for their coaching staffs.

When comparing the amount of money going to all of the assistant coaching stipends for the ninth through twelfth grade programs combined, there are four schools at the low end of the range. Independence (North Carolina), Lakeland (Florida), and Miami Northwestern (Florida) each combine for less than twenty thousand dollars distributed amongst their entire assistant coaching staffs. The fourth school, Central Catholic (Pennsylvania), combines for just under twenty-three thousand dollars that is distributed among all of their assistant football coaches.

De La Salle (California), South Panola (Mississippi) and Colerain (Ohio) are in the second tier of financial support. De La Salle employs twelve paid coaches who each receive between five hundred and five thousand dollars. The assistant coaches at Colerain combine to earn $39,200, which is at least double of both of the Florida schools and Independence (North Carolina). South Panola (Mississippi) helps pay the offensive and defensive coordinators more money by having them on twelve month teaching contracts instead of the traditional ten month contract. It is difficult to pin down a specific number with regard to how much money is paid to South Panola assistant coaches as some of the extra money is tied into teaching salaries.

The third tier of schools includes Katy (Texas), Carroll (Texas), and Jenks (Oklahoma). The Katy assistant coaches combine to earn around sixty-six thousand dollars for coaching football. The eighteen Carroll High School coaches in Southlake, Texas get paid seventy-five hundred dollars for coaching football *and* one other sport. If forty-five hundred dollars of the seventy-five hundred dollars is for coaching football, the total amount for the Carroll assistant coaches would total around eighty-one thousand dollars. The assistant coaches at Jenks combine to make eighty-three thousand dollars. With coaching stipends or supplements over eighty thousand dollars, the head coaches of these programs can have the luxury of having assistant coaching positions that pay assistant coaches more money, thus potentially attracting more highly qualified coaches. It might be even more important to note that they are able to have much larger coaching staffs with minimal volunteers. While volunteer coaches are bonuses to most programs, schools that have more paid coaches will often have more coaches on the staff with full commitment levels.

The school that stands out on its own is Lowndes High School in Valdosta, Georgia. The amount of money that goes to pay coaches in the ninth through twelfth grade program at Lowndes is $150,820. A ninth grade coach at Lowndes makes more money than the head varsity coach at Lakeland (Florida), Miami Northwestern (Florida), and Independence (North Carolina) when just the coaching stipends are compared. A ninth grade coach at Lowndes earns around five thousand dollars. A varsity position coach at Lowndes makes around nine thousand dollars each season. An offensive or defensive coordinator at Lowndes will make around fourteen thousand dollars. What may be even more eye-opening is the amount of money that each middle school coaching staff makes as they prepare students for Lowndes High School football. Each of the two middle school coaching staffs combines to make $18,750. Amazingly, the Lowndes middle schools each have around the same amount of money for coaches as the two Florida schools and Independence High School in North Carolina. Evangel High School in Shreveport, Louisiana determines each coach's salary based on need; this is determined between the chancellor of the school and each individual coach. As a result, it is difficult to compare Evangel with the rest of the schools.

When comparing some of the salaries and stipends for the head coaches, there is a significant disparity amongst the head coaches in this book as well. The stipend for being a head football coach at Lakeland High School (Florida) is $3,974 for the fall football season. At Miami Northwestern (Florida), the pay is similar with the head coach earning $3,090 for the fall season. Coaches at both Florida schools make additional money for coaching spring football. For example the head football coach at Miami Northwestern earns an additional $1,659 for the twenty days of spring football. In the same ballpark as the two Florida High Schools falls Independence (North Carolina). The stipend for the head football coach at Independence High School is $3,900. The head coach is also on an eleven month annual contract instead of the normal ten month contract. This allows the head coach to make an extra month's salary as well. This is common practice in the state of North Carolina.

The stipend for the head football Coach at Colerain High School (Ohio) will be $7,200 in 2008, which is $1,000 shy of what the Central Catholic (Pennsylvania) head coach makes for his position. The stipend for the head football coaching position at Jenks (Oklahoma) is $15,000. In a 2005, a research article was written by the, "Austin American-Statesman" comparing Texas high school coaches' salaries. The numbers in that article compared the total amount of money each coach made regardless of how it was broken up. In 2005, according to the article, the head football coach at Katy (Texas) made $79,240 a year, and the head football coach at Carroll High School in Southlake, Texas made $90,510 a year.

When looking at all twelve programs one can see that dynasties are built with vast differences in funding for coaching staffs. Yet, these spans don't necessarily make or break programs. It seems that the financial resources are but one ingredient in the successes of high school football teams. When comparing the price tags that come with each team, it would be fair to say that higher paid salaries don't always equate to more success.

Conclusion

THROUGHOUT MY EXAMINATION of these twelve phenomenal programs, I have been fortunate enough to have such in-depth looks into these programs in order to uncover the similarities and the differences. There were three common notions that were dispelled after comparing and contrasting all of the schools. Firstly, though lofty financial resources produce elaborate stadiums, huge coaching staffs, extravagant facilities, and massive booster clubs, having access to excessive funds didn't factor into even half of these twelve paramount programs. Though generous financial resources are a bonus to a program, they are clearly not vital for building a gridiron dynasty. Secondly, these schools proved that a vibrant youth football program within their communities isn't always necessary in building a gridiron dynasty. Even though a youth program can be advantageous for many teams, half of the schools compared here evidenced that a gridiron dynasty can be assembled without one. Lastly, rosters that pump out large numbers of Division One players are not necessarily widespread amongst these programs. While individual talent is clearly beneficial, it is not what defines these programs as *elite.*

All of these programs had common threads that were definite attributes to the power of their programs. One thing that these programs illustrated was that they were much more than just players and coaches striving to excel. Each of these schools contains a unique community effort geared for rising to the top of their game. The commitment level of the athletes and coaches was generally equitable with the members of their school administrations, parents, and community members. These selected programs often surpass others in part because their communities place a great importance on the development of student athletes within their football programs.

Next, while all twelve head coaches employ varying methods in building top notch programs, they are all unified in holding clear visions and tactics for building dominating teams. They are methodical in the approaches taken to rise to the pinnacle of high school football. All twelve of these coaches place high values on assistant coaches who demonstrate loyalty and willingness to move in sync with the direction of their football programs.

Additionally, each of the twelve programs has proven that competing on the national level requires an excellent strength and conditioning program. While the specifics of each of the strength and conditioning programs differ, all of the schools place tremendous importance on their strength and conditioning programs; they all recognize the added edge this adds to achieving success. With the tremendous depth developed within the strength and conditioning programs, nearly all of these schools have very few players playing on both offense and defense; this permits the athletes and coaches to specialize on one side of the football. The results of this come in the form of strong teams capable of wearing down opponents and dominating the kicking game.

Another common theme amongst all of the programs is the huge emphasis on team building. Once again, this is an area where coaches each have their own distinctive styles of uniting individuals into a tightly formed group. Though their approaches differentiate while achieving the objective of unification, this notion of team building rests at the very center of comprehending how these programs can compete at such high levels year after year.

Finally, the only common denominator in regard to offense and defense comes in the imperative emphasis placed on running the football. While only a few of these programs pass the football at a high level, all of these programs run the football effectively. Some might argue that this is the least important of all of the common denominators, yet it proves that as the game of football continues to evolve; the best high school football programs across the nation still run the football.

As I look back on the journey I've taken to compile this book, I feel honored to have had the opportunities to sit down with some of the best high school football coaches in America and listen to the wisdom that they've gathered throughout their coaching careers. This whole process was nothing short of incredible for me. I will be forever grateful to the coaches who took the time out of their very busy schedules to help me view their programs from their perspectives and philosophies. These men have not only inspired and guided entire communities in the processes of building gridiron dynasties, but more importantly, they have made lifetime impacts on the athletes who were privileged to at one point in time call them, "Coach".

Appendix

Carroll Dragons

This smash route is clearly the most foundational passing play for the Carroll Dragons. They run this route out of Trips as well as Empty formations. Here in a balanced formation the quarterback is simply reading the cornerback to his right. If the cornerback doesn't cover the hitch the ball immediately goes to the outside receiver who runs the hitch. If the cornerback takes away the hitch now the quarterback gets his eyes on the safeties. If the slot receiver to the right who is running the corner has beat the strong safety the ball goes to him at a 22 yard landmark with the corner route. If the safeties are playing really wide taking away the corner route the quarterback then looks to throw the seam from the backside slot receiver. Lastly, the backside wide receiver has some type of man beater route on that the quarterback will look to in the event of an unprotected blitz.

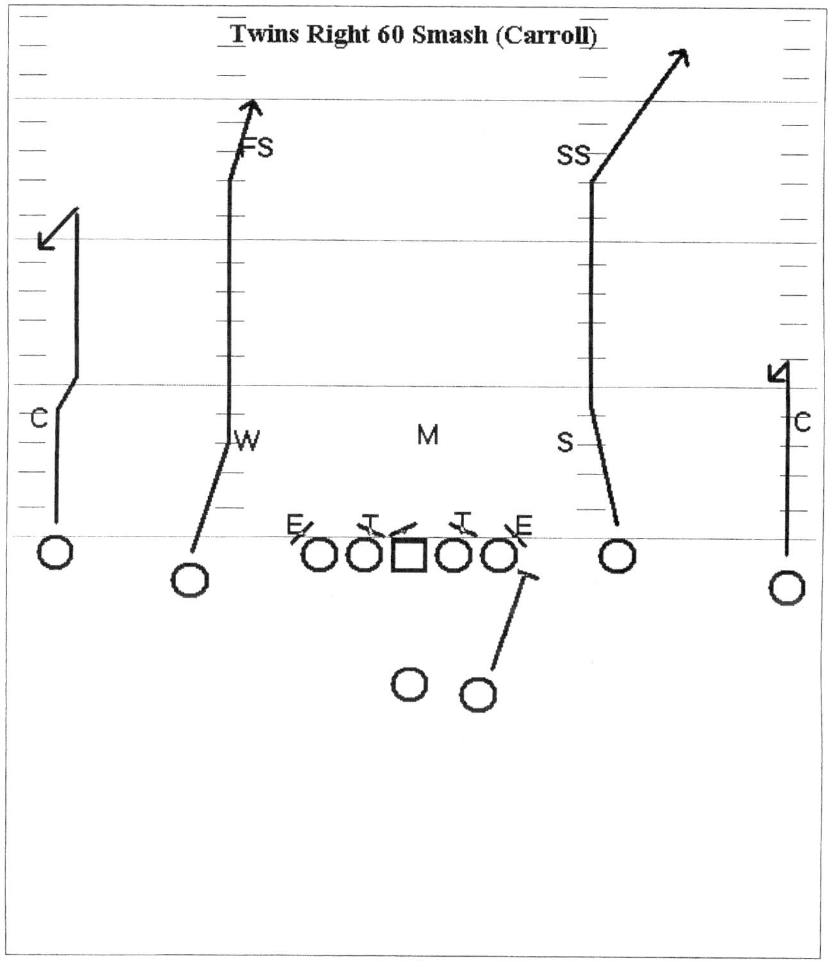
Twins Right 60 Smash (Carroll)
FS
SS
C
W
M
S
C
E
T
T
E

Central Catholic Vikings

The Counter is a big way that the Vikings impose their physical brand of football on their opponents. The fullback fills in the B Gap out. The playside tight end, tackle, and guard all block their inside gaps up to a second level player. The center fills for the pulling guard. This play could hit outside if the defensive end squeezes down.

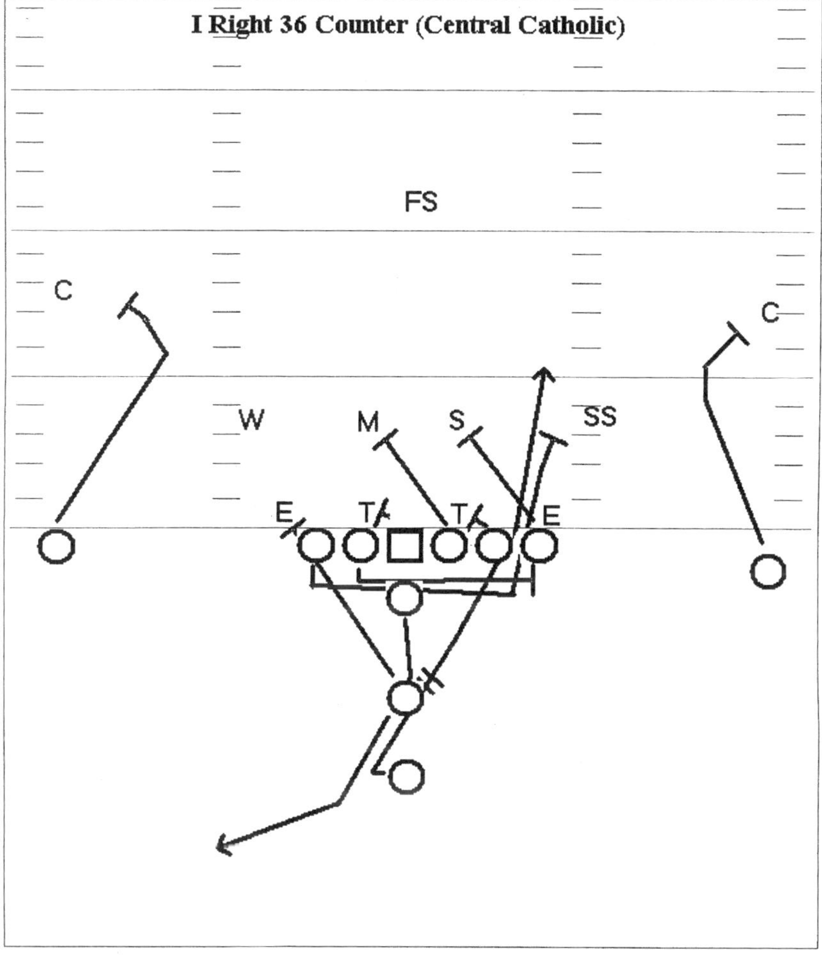
I Right 36 Counter (Central Catholic)
FS
C
C
W
M
S
SS
E
T
T
E

Colerain Cardinals

The Colerain offense is in a large part built around the Triple Option. Here against a 4-4 Defense the first read for the quarterback is the playside defensive end who is one of two players that are unblocked on this play. As the ball is inserted into the fullback the quarterback has his eyes on the playside defensive end. If the defensive end does not come down to tackle the fullback the fullback will keep the football. If the defensive end comes down and tackles the fullback the quarterback will pull the ball out and get his eyes on the strong safety. If the strong safety takes the quarterback the ball will be pitched to the slotback. If the strong safety takes the slotback the quarterback will then keep the ball. This foundational play that Colerain runs out of a variety of formations forces defenses to be disciplined and play assignment football.

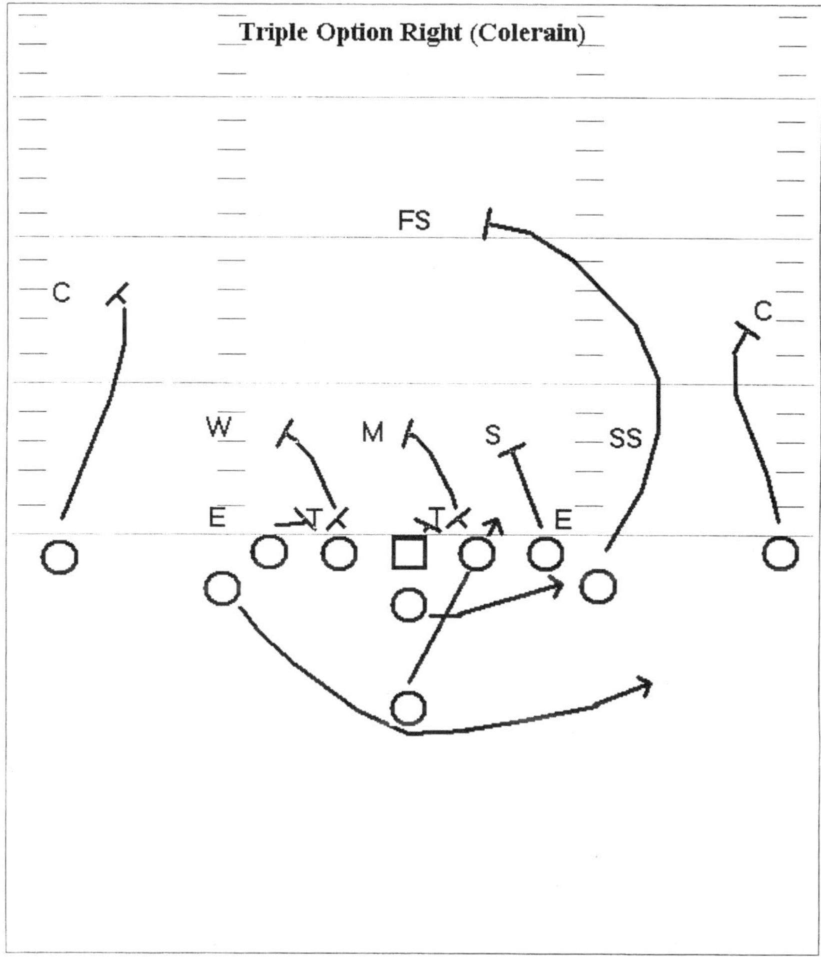
Triple Option Right (Colerain)
FS
C
C
W
M
S
SS
E
T
T
E

De La Salle Spartans

The Power play was a foundational play for the duration of their 151 game winning streak. This play was very difficult to defend for linebackers who read the action of the backfield. The play side guard, tackle, and tight end all block a down lineman in their inside gap and then work up to a linebacker if there is not a down lineman in their gap. The center fills backside and the fullback fills for the pulling tackle. Maurice Jones-Drew now with the Jacksonville Jaguars was almost impossible to defend on this play.

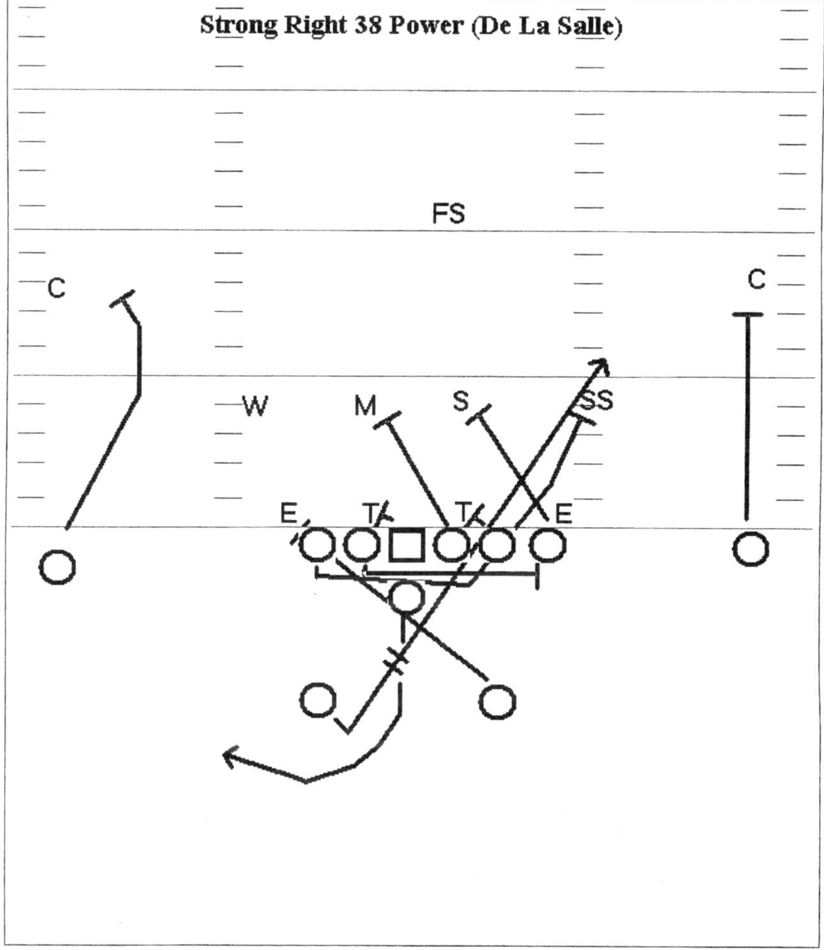
Strong Right 38 Power (De La Salle)
FS
C
C
W
M
S
SS
E
T
T
E

Evangel Eagles

Interestingly, Evangel names their receivers from left to right, LTYR. This stands for left to your right. The Evangel offense is based on a numbering system. On this play the quarterback is nine yards deep in his shotgun, which is unique to the Evangel offense. Evangel likes to throw the ball down the field so the quarterback can attack either cornerback vertically if he likes the matchup. If the quarterback chooses to work inside with the slot receivers he simply reads the free safety and throws the deep in or the post over the top depending on what the free safety does.

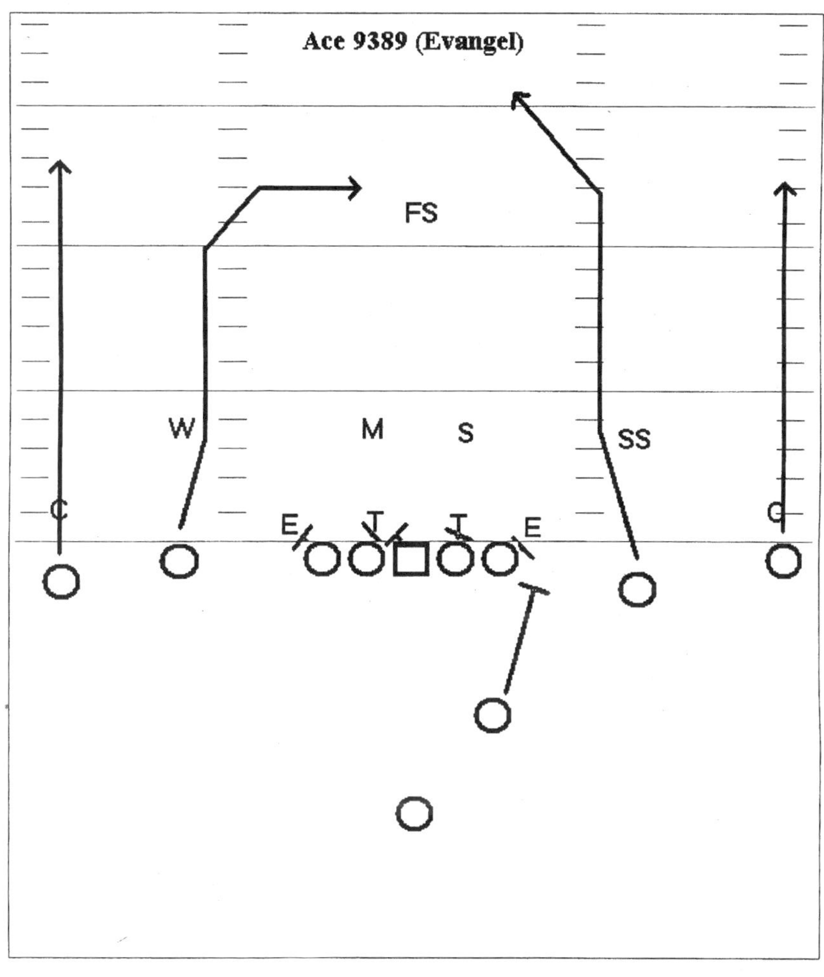
Ace 9389 (Evangel)
FS
W
M
S
SS
C
E
T
T
E
C

Independence Patriots

The Independence Patriots will look backside at the virtual one on one matchup versus cover three teams. If the quarterback chooses to work the three receiver side of this route he will first read the cornerback. If the corner sinks to play the corner route the ball will either go to the swing or the hitch depending on how the strong safety plays. If the free safety cheats out of the middle of the field the ball will go to the tight end up the seam.

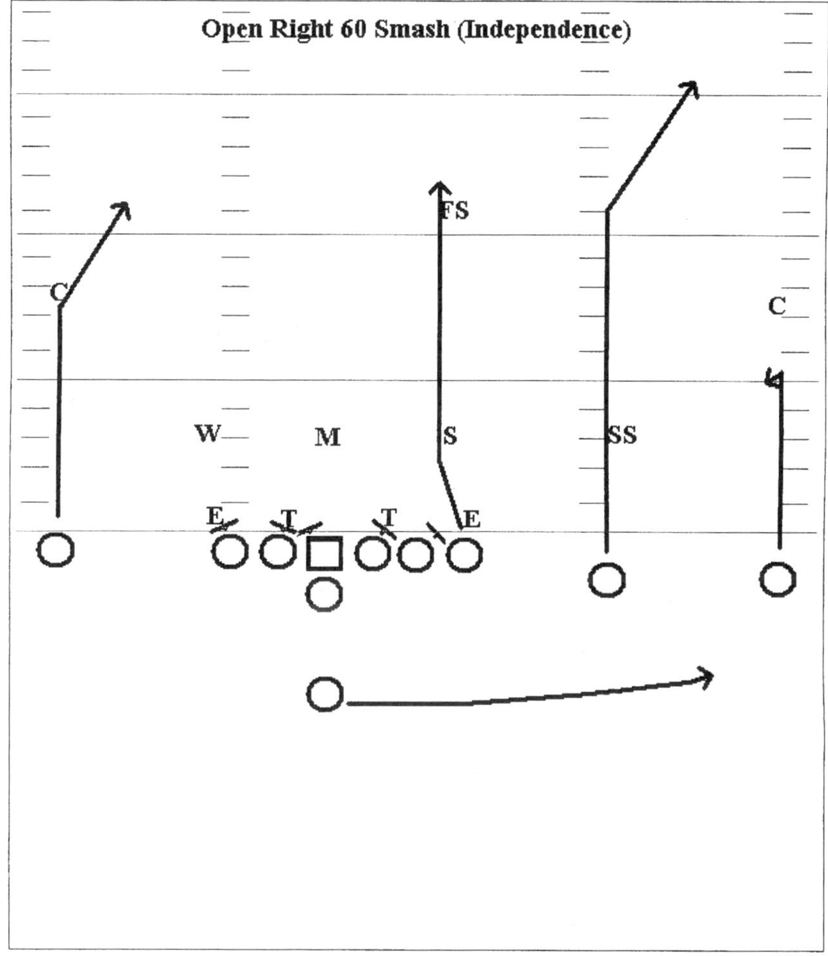
Open Right 60 Smash (Independence)
FS
C
C
W
M
S
SS
E
T
T
E

Jenks Trojans

The bread and butter route for Jenks is their Scat route. The Trojans were very efficient throwing this route over the last two seasons. In 2006, Jenks completed 77% of these routes, and in 2007 the offense completed 79%. Additionally, in the 2006 State Championship game they completed all seven Scat routes they attempted. A variation of this route is used by Jenks out of a wide range of formations including two back sets. The slot receiver is aligned four yards from the tight end and the wide receiver is four yards from the slot. The slot receiver has what Jenks calls a Cop route. The Cop route is simply a corner or a post depending on the coverage. If the middle of the field is open in a two safety high look the slot will run a post. If the quarterback and safety see a single safety look he will run a corner. The quarterback first gets his eyes on the cornerback. If the corner sinks to take care of the slot receivers corner route the quarterback quickly gets his eyes on the strong safety. If the safety takes away the swing by the running back the quarterback looks to throw the pivot to the wide receiver. If the strong linebacker takes away the pivot, the quarterback then looks to throw the pivot to the tight end. Jenks will tag whatever route they want to with the backside receiver. Against a man pressure team the backside receiver will become more of an option.

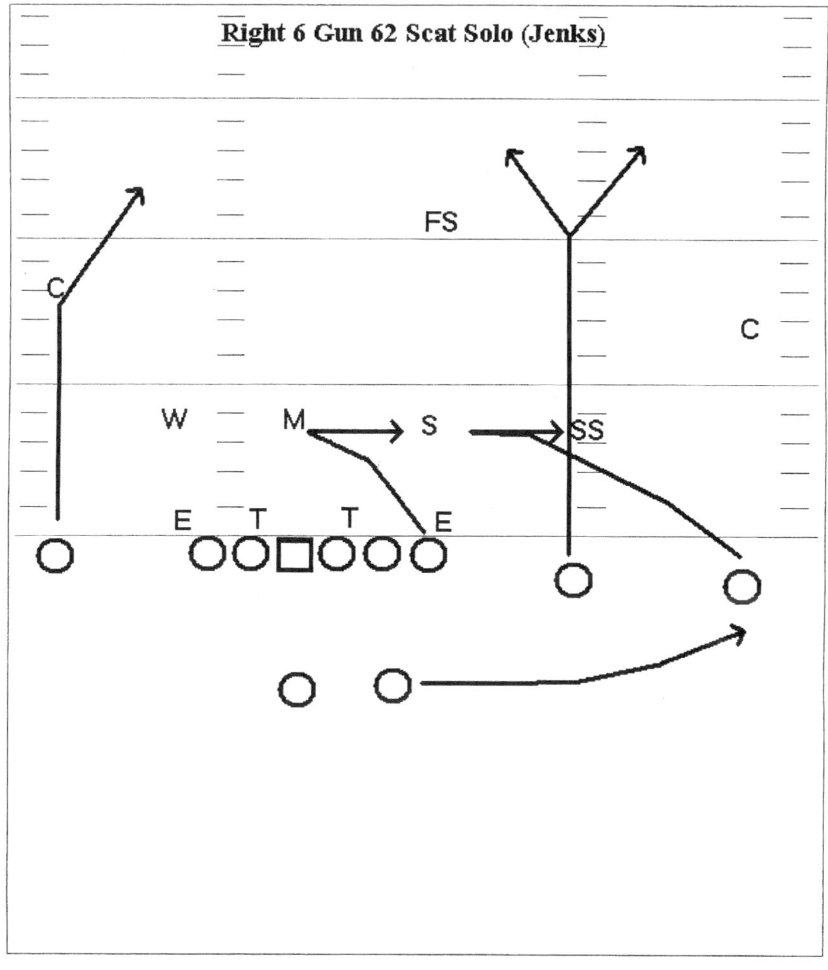
Right 6 Gun 62 Scat Solo (Jenks)
FS
C
C
W
M
S
SS
E
T
T
E

Katy Tigers

The Katy Tigers have made a living off of the traditional Power Play. They will run this play both strong and weak. The playside blocking scheme is gap down and up for the guard, tackle, and tight end. The center fills backside for the pulling guard and the fullback kicks out the end. The backside guard is then pulling up the hole for the first defender he sees. Against an even front Katy will block out with the tight end and the play becomes more of an inside play.

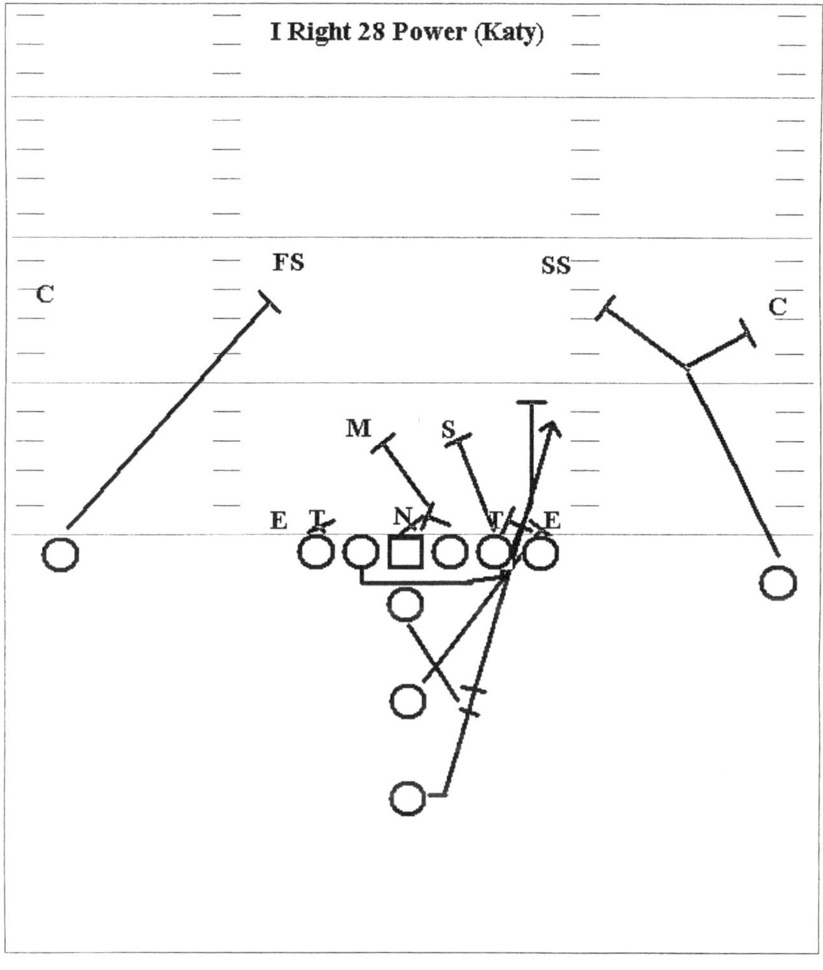
I Right 28 Power (Katy)
FS
SS
C
C
M
S
E
T
N
T
E

Lakeland Dreadnaughts

The 30 Trap option was a play that averaged close to ten yards a play for Lakeland over the years. The play appears to be a triple option but in reality the play call eliminates the fullback from ever getting the football. The quarterback uses the same footwork as on a Midline running play and the fullback is heading directly down the midline. The quarterback then proceeds down the line where he reads the unblocked defensive end to determine whether to keep or pitch. Lakeland was extremely successful with this play when they had a very physical slot receiver who could block the linebacker lined up over him.

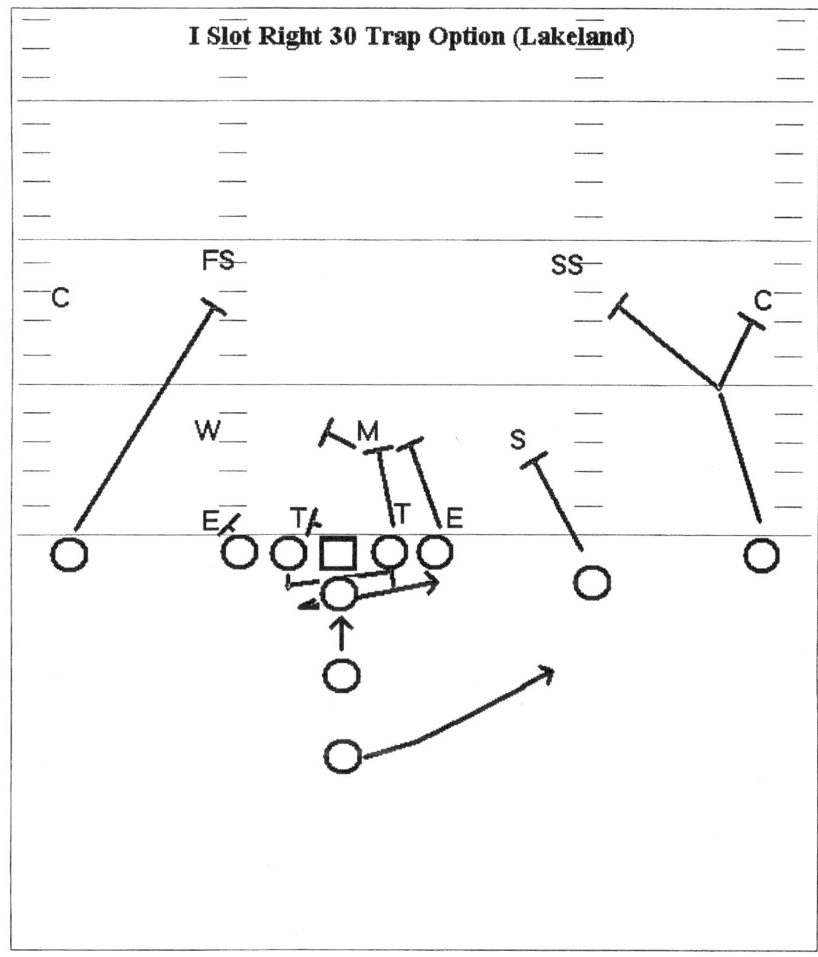
I Slot Right 30 Trap Option (Lakeland)
FS
SS
C
C
W
M
S
E
T
T
E

Lowndes Vikings

The Buck Sweep is as foundational to Lowndes as it is to other Wing T teams. A good mesh point with the quarterback and fullback is a key so that the linebackers have a tough time determining who has the football. The guards need to be athletic as both pull on this play. The playside guard kicks out the defensive end, while the backside guard pulls up for the first defender he sees. The playside tackle, tight end, and wingback all block down on this play. Lowndes runs this play as well as any high school team in the nation.

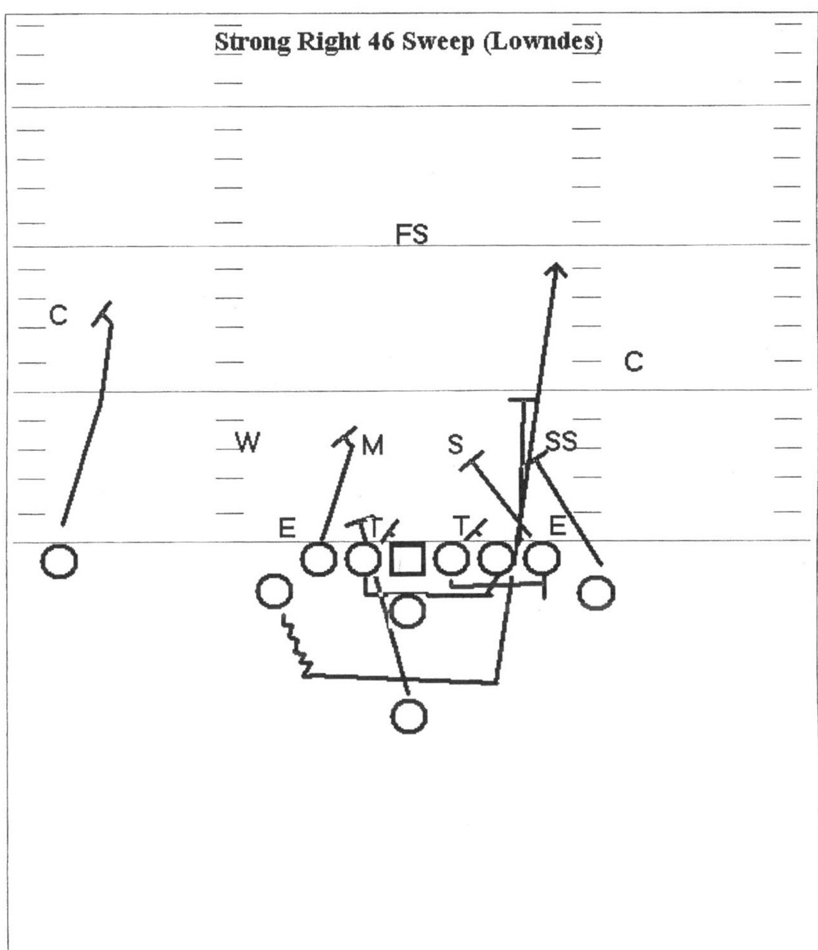
Strong Right 46 Sweep (Lowndes)
FS
C
C
W
M
S
SS
E
T
T
E

South Panola Tigers

The South Panola Tigers love to run the inside zone running play. They run this out of a variety of formations. In this zone blocking scheme the play could stay playside or cut back. The ball carrier is reading the three technique and determining to cut back based on how this defender plays. The quarterback is responsible for holding the backside end with his fake.

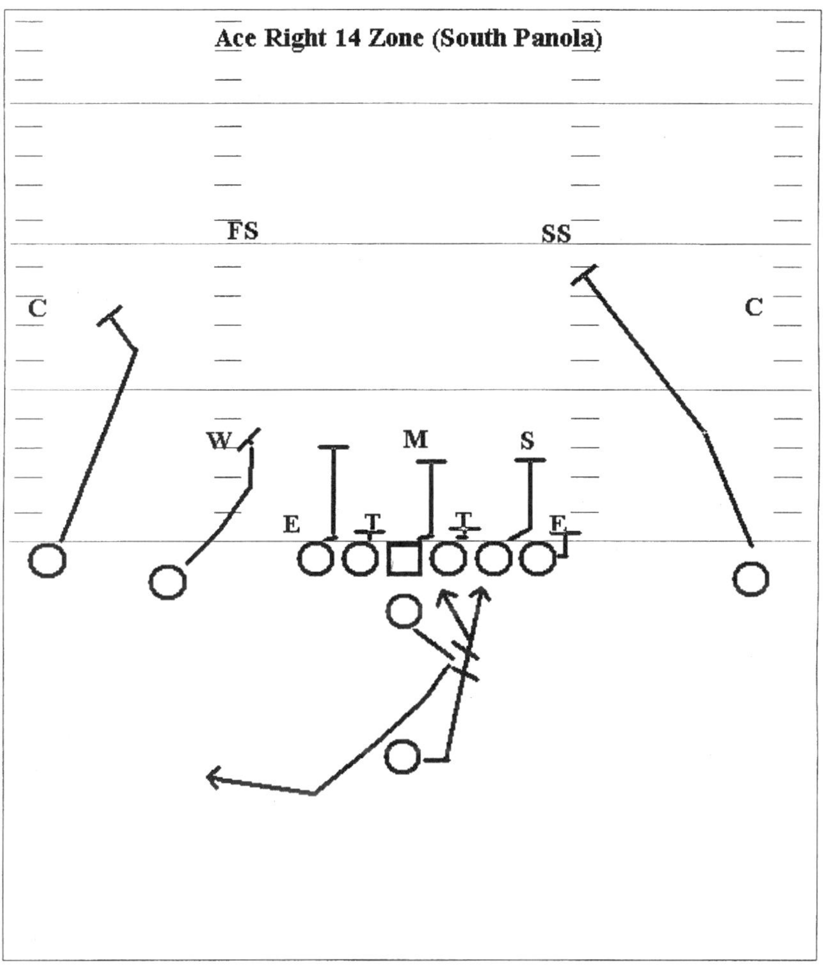
Ace Right 14 Zone (South Panola)
FS
SS
C
C
W
M
S
E
T
T
E

References

1. Allick, Earl. Personal interview. February 2008.
2. Bachman, John. Personal interview. April 2008.
3. Baker, Matt. "Jenks-Union hits big time, crowds follow," *Tulsa World*, 05 September 2007. www.tulsaworld.com/sports/extra/atricle.aspx?tab=hs&articleid=070905_2_B1_hOnce61141 (February 2008).
4. "Big 33 Buddies," http://big33.org/buddies.htm (February 2008).
5. "Big 33 Game History," http://big33.org/gamehistory.htm (February 2008).
6. Bolden, Tom. Personal interview. February 2008.
7. Brady, Erik. "Carroll-Northwestern match shaped by contrasts," *USA Today*, 13 September 2007. www.usatoday.com/sports/preps/football/2007-09-13-carroll-northwestern_N.htm (March 2008).
8. "Burger King Ohio vs. USA Challenge set for Labor Day Weekend," 27 July 2007 www.ohiovsusa.com/bkherbstreitpressrelease072707.pdf (February 2008).
9. Castle, Bill. Personal interview. February 2008.
10. "Central Catholic Football Program," 2005.
11. Charles Crummie, "Coach Salaries," (April 11, 2008), Personal email (11 April 2008).
12. "Coaching Salaries for Classes 5A, 4A." http://alt.coxnewsweb.com/statesman/pdf/coaching_salaries.pdf (February 2008).
13. Cobb, Mike. "And Then There Was Football." www.lakelandfootball.com/history.htm (February 2008).
14. Doherty, Tim. "Easterling ready for scrutiny after high school sex arrest," *USA Today*, 26 July 2007. www.**usatoday**.com/sports/college/football/c**usa**/2007-07-26-**easterling**-scrutiny_N.htm (February 2008).
15. "Famous Alumni," *Wikipedia*. http://en.wikipedia.org/wiki/Miami_Northwestern_High_School (March 2008).
16. Jones-Drew, Maurice. Personal interview. April 2008.
17. Johnson, Hiram. Personal interview. March 2008.
18. Joseph, Gary. Personal interview. April 2008.

19. Knotts, Tom. Personal interview. March 2008.
20. Ladouceur, Bob. Personal interview. April 2008.
21. Lawlor, Christopher. "Miami Northwestern goes wire-to-wire as No. 1,"16 December 2007. www.sports.espn.go.com/ncaa/highschool/news/story?id=3157098(March 2008).
22. Lee, Aaron S. "Breaking the Mold: The truth behind the success of Evangel Christian Academy football," *American Football Monthly*, 02 October 2002. www.americanfootballmonthly.com/Subaccess/Magazine/2002/oct02/spotlight04.html (13 April 2008).
23. Luna, Jack. Phone Interview. May 2008.
24. Malone, Christian. "Coaches: 1-AAAAA a great football region," 29 July 2007. www.valdostadailytimes.com/sports/local_story_210043323.html (February 2008).
25. McPherson, Randy. Personal interview. March 2008.
26. National Football: National Rankings, National Leaders. www.maxpreps.com/FanPages/NatFOOTBALL.mxp (February 2008).
27. Navarro, Manny. "Winning game plan recharges Miami Northwestern," *Miami Herald*, 04 October 2007. www.miamiherald.com/295/story/259669.html (February 2008).
28. Pogue, Lance. Personal interview. April 2008.
29. Robertson, Linda. "Business Trip? Bulls can't forget to have fun," Miami Herald, 13 September 2007. www.miamiherald.com (March 2008).
30. Rolle, Billy. Personal interview. February 2008.
31. Scholarship information. www.scout.com (February 2008).
32. School eNews Online. "Public Bond Meeting Scheduled," 6 January 2006. www.southlakecarroll.edu/enews1.6.06.htm#superintendent
33. "Super 25 Rankings," *USA Today*. 26 December 2007, www.usatoday.com/sports/preps/rankingsindex.htm (January 2008).
34. Totten, Terry. Personal interview. February 2008.
35. Trimble, Allen. Personal interview. March 2008.
36. Trosclair, Carroll. "Miami Northwestern edges Southlake Carroll in battle for top ranking," 17 September 2007. http://football.suite101.com/article.cfm/high_school_football (February 2008).
37. Wasson, Hal. Personal interview. April 2008.
38. Year of the Bull. Todd Lubin. DVD. Animus Films and Lasu Productions, 2003.

About the Author

Gavin Kralik grew up in Sumner, Washington before going on to play as a wide receiver at Liberty University. He served as a co-captain there in 2000, and led Liberty in receiving in 1999 and 2000. Kralik then earned his Masters in Education from Liberty University in 2001. Today, at the age of 31, he is the Head Football Coach at Bethel High School in Spanaway, Washington. He and his wife, Krista, have three children and are expecting a fourth child in September of 2008.